Praise for *No-Drama Leadership* and Marlene Chism

"Selected as one of the best business books of 2015 by Soundview Executive Book Summaries."

—Soundview Executive Book Summaries

"Marlene Chism shows leaders how to redirect negative energy into positive action. The No-Drama leader creates a culture that delivers results, and keeps everyone aligned with noble purpose."

—Lisa Earle McLeod, Forbes.com columnist and author of the best-seller, *Selling with Noble Purpose*

"Marlene Chism has a powerful way of communicating with readers. Her insights on what today's leaders need and what is expected of them is conveyed in this book. Instant enlightenment. Guaranteed!"

—Babitha Balakrishnan, senior editor of Excellence Essentials Publications with HR.Com, the largest global social networking and resource site for HR Professionals

"Workplace drama compromises morale, jeopardizes productivity, and encourages turnover because star performers simply won't put up with it. Marlene Chism understands that only leaders can truly stop it and prevent it before it destroys the organization's culture. Leaders who commit to growing profits and playing a bigger game should read and heed Chism's advice."

—Linda D. Henman, owner Henman Performance Group and author of *Challenge the Ordinary*

"Marlene knows her stuff! If you are ready to look at your management difficulties as an opportunity to develop and improve, then this book is for you. We think it is very People Centric!"

—Don Harkey and Randy Mayes, founders of People Centric Consulting Group

"Talk to some managers for any length of time, and you'll hear them describe a typical day with words like *busy*, *stressed*, or even *burned out*. But when you speak with an enlightened leader, you hear words like *aware*, *aligned*, and *accountable*. How it possible that bosses within the same organization can range from feeling like *helpless victims* to *enlightened, engaged leaders?* Marlene Chism's **No-Drama Leadership** shows leaders how to step out from under the shadow of drama and into enlightenment."

—Scott Carbonara, aka The Leadership Therapist, and author of *A Manager's Guide to Employee Engagement*

"*Marlene* Chism has hit the nail on the head. We need to get this book not only into the hands of corporate America but also in public safety and government. **No-Drama Leadership** will change the way we do business."

—Kenny Mountain, president & CEO, Combix 911 Specialists

"Marlene Chism demystifies drama like no other. Stop letting your culture fall victim to drama; instead, become an enlightened leader who aligns your team through values-based actions. **No-Drama Leadership** provides leaders with the most comprehensive and simple approach to deconstruct drama and build a flourishing culture—in any industry or situation."

—Jocelyn Godfrey, president, Spiritus Communications

"Every leader who reads this book will immediately relate to the problems that so often go with leadership. Marlene does a masterful job **in No-Drama Leadership** of taking the reader from pain and frustration into hope and excitement by understanding and correcting the role that the leader plays in workplace drama."

—Bonnie Hagemann, CEO, Executive Development Associates, Inc.

NO-DRAMA
LEADERSHIP

NO-DRAMA LEADERSHIP

*How Enlightened Leaders Transform
Culture in the Workplace*

MARLENE CHISM

First published by Bibliomotion, Inc.
39 Harvard Street
Brookline, MA 02445
Tel: 617-934-2427
www.bibliomotion.com

Printed in the United States of America

Library of Congress Cataloging-in-Publication Data

Chism, Marlene.
  No-drama leadership : how enlightened leaders transform culture in the workplace / Marlene Chism. — First Edition.
      pages cm
  Summary: "No-Drama Leadership aims to influence corporate and organizational leaders to recognize the impact of changing times resulting in the need to place priority on a new type of leadership development that focuses not only on the outer game of results but on the inner game of leadership growth" — Provided by publisher.
  ISBN 978-1-62956-061-8 (hardback) — ISBN 978-1-62956-062-5 (ebook) — ISBN 978-1-62956-063-2 (enhanced ebook) *5661 2715* *05/15*
  1. Leadership. 2. Communication in organizations. I. Title.
  HD57.7.C5163 2015
  658.4'092—dc23

                              2015000883

To all who have the courage to lead

CONTENTS

Contents

PART 3

The Power to Create

INTRODUCTION

In January of 2012 I got a call from Heather, a public safety manager at her wits' end. "I feel like I'm in a black hole and can't get out. The supervisors are not performing well, and I don't know how to help them. They hint instead of giving direction. The employees are confused and frustrated. There's no accountability, feedback, or discipline,"[1] she said. Heather's time was spent listening to gossip and complaints through her open door, which had turned into a revolving door. Morale was low, absenteeism was on the rise, and the budget was taking a nosedive due to employee turnover.

After reading my first book, *Stop Workplace Drama*,[2] Heather reached out to me, seeking help and mentoring she could not get from her workplace. Top leaders do not understand that the lack of development for supervisors and managers contributes to most of the cultural problems in the workplace: low morale, ineffective performance, absenteeism, and turnover. At the root of these problems are leadership deficiencies, including supervisors' failure to build and maintain good workplace relationships.

Workplace Relationships

According to Gallup, the number-one reason employees leave a job is because of their dysfunctional relationship with direct supervisors.[3] It's not lack of technical training, intelligence, or capacity to lead that fosters relationship problems. It's poor leadership development.

Most new leaders do not know how to redirect negativity or how to deal with complaining. They spend needless hours fixing employee issues instead of coaching employees to take responsibility. They avoid difficult conversations about performance, and they often make promises they cannot deliver. These bad habits contribute to a culture of mistrust and disempowerment. Perhaps the reason there is a blind spot from the top layer is that no matter how many challenges new leaders face, very few have the courage or confidence to ask for help, fearing that they will be seen as incompetent or ineffective.

Very few newly promoted first- and second-level leaders come with the skills they need to be effective leaders. Yet very little leadership development is offered. It's common practice for companies to promote a good technical performer to a supervisory management position without ever training him in the character development or leadership skills necessary to shift his identity from "one of them" to "one of us." In fact, a report by Deloitte Consulting and Bersin by Deloitte, entitled *Global Human Capital Trends 2014*, found that first-level managers receive the lowest per-person share of leadership development resources.[4]

In Heather's case, she skipped the first-level supervisory position. Instead, she was promoted straight into management after only three years of experience. Her training consisted of two days with the former manager. On day one, her predecessor told Heather how to pay invoices. After lunch she got a tour of the equipment room and computer networks. On day two, Heather hopped into her former manager's car for a ride around the county while she said her good-byes. On day three, Heather was in charge. When she called me, it was *ten years* later.

Most leaders have no idea how their behaviors contribute to the workplace drama they experience daily. Almost every manager

I have worked with thinks the problem is the supervisors he manages, and every supervisor I've worked with thinks the problem is the employees he supervises. The finger pointing doesn't stop there. The higher-level executives also think the problem is everyone else.

I don't care if it's the senior vice president of a multibillion-dollar company or a mom-and-pop small business owner, when a leader has workplace drama she always thinks it's about Stephanie, Kadin, Kim or Antonio, and never about the leadership.

It's time for an awakening. I call it No-Drama Leadership.

No-Drama Leadership

My first book, *Stop Workplace Drama*, was written for those who simply don't get any leadership development. These first level supervisors and managers are the ones who work in the trenches every day dealing with the workplace drama—the gossip, backstabbing, power struggles, low morale, lack of engagement, poor team coordination, insubordination, absenteeism, and turnover. No matter what kind of label you put on it, it's all drama, and drama is always viewed as an obstacle to peace and prosperity.

These first- and second-level leaders are caught in the middle between frontline employees and upper management. They are often disconnected from the big picture and how their leadership connects with the company's mission, vision, and organizational strategies. *Stop Workplace Drama* gave these leaders an overview of what contributes to drama as well as the practical skills to put a stop to the drama—the obstacle to their sanity and productivity (peace and prosperity).

This book builds a bridge *between* the levels of leadership while offering a multifaceted perspective. Top leaders can now tap into the mind-sets and viewpoints from all levels—from the eyes of the employees to the supervisors to the managers inside the company. And first-level leaders—supervisors and managers—can read this book and learn how to see things from the executive's point of view. My hope is that the dialogues that come from reading together can help colleagues at all levels in the company work together to achieve the greater good.

No-Drama Leadership introduces a new model for leadership: it changes the language and considers everyone a leader. Seeing managers, supervisors, and frontline employees as leaders encourages people at all levels to grow and learn from one another. This shift creates an identity transformation needed in today's rapidly changing environment.

This book contrasts two perspectives: one of drama and one of enlightenment. While the drama perspective is about seeing obstacles, the enlightened perspective is about seeing opportunities. Thus, the enlightened leader has *"the eyes to see"* how obstacles (drama) offer rich opportunities for leadership growth.

It's time to leave the drama perspective behind and enter a new age of enlightenment. The language from the drama perspective is oriented toward excuses, justifications, lack of empowerment, and a void of leadership responsibility. Listen to the language of those around you to hear whether your company has a culture of No-Drama Leadership. Ask a leader within your company why she avoided a difficult conversation. If you hear something like, "The employee has ten years' seniority" or "I inherited the problem from the last manager" or "That person was recovering from a difficult situation at home and the timing was off," you know your leaders are working from the drama perspective.

A leader with a drama perspective asks, "How do I supervise, manipulate, or transfer Cary, Caleb, or Chris?" The leader with an enlightened perspective asks a different question: "What can Cary, Caleb, or Chris teach me about my leadership weaknesses?" No-Drama Leaders take responsibility for their language, using communication not as a soft skill but as a strategy, learning the necessary mind-sets and processes to get results, as I will show later.

No-Drama Leadership is about building a culture of enlightened leaders who are aware, aligned, and accountable. These leaders have the "Super Vision" to forecast, to see problems before they metastasize into multimillion-dollar lawsuits, wasted energy, and lost productivity.

Why We Need Enlightened Leaders

Employees of the Market Basket grocery chain made history in 2014 when they went on strike to protest the firing of their beloved CEO, Arthur T. Demoulas. What's fascinating about this case is not only the speed at which the protest was organized but the way in which it was organized and the support it garnered. Once employee organizers created wearemarketbasket.com and a Face book page (which, at this writing, had more than ninety thousand likes), change ignited. While the board originally planned to make more profits by ousting Arthur T., it, in effect, lost more than $10 million a day for six weeks because employees decided they had the power to choose differently.

There was no union to organize the strike, just enough dedicated workers with longevity who were completely engaged and committed to the mission and vision of Market Basket. Customers and vendors supported the strike. Eventually the board gave in, and Arthur T. went back to work with all the previously fired managers and on-strike workers.

What can we learn from the Market Basket episode? Power is shifting. The speed at which change can happen is astounding. People wield power through social media, and, as a result, transparency is no longer an option—it is a given. People at the bottom have more choices, and they are waking up to the power their choices provide. When people believe in a purpose, they will sacrifice everything to stand up for what they believe in. The Market Basket episode is a snapshot of what is to come. People are ready for transformational change. They will demand enlightenment in their leadership. Speed, power, transparency, choice. These are the reasons we need enlightened leaders.

Speed: We want more speed, but we don't have the experience to handle it. We are all driving race cars without the experience or expertise needed to prevent a tragic accident. Most of us are overwhelmed every day. Each time-saving device we acquire brings with it the added pressure of increased expectations for immediacy. From letters to e-mails to texts, the faster the information comes in, the faster it has to go back out.

When driving a race car, the faster you go, the greater the danger. The faster you go, the less time you have to think about your response. Increases in cyberbullying, road rage, and acts of violence suggest that peoples' fuses are getting shorter. We train our brains to be impatient, irreverent, and uncivil. We are swiftly losing that space between stimulus and response, yet instead of taking a breath, we wish to move even faster.

Leadership impact: Because of speed, leaders must learn how to manage the emotions that come with unexpected and unwanted change, while modeling self-control and reducing mental and emotional overload in the workplace. In addition, the need for leadership development and training is going to increase. According to the *Human Capital Trends Report for 2014,* produced by Deloitte Consulting and Bersin by Deloitte, "In a world where knowledge doubles every year and skills have a half-life of 2.5–5 years, leaders need constant development."[5] What we learn today is out of date three years later. Leaders need to take initiative for their own development, as well as take opportunities offered by the company.

Power: For the first time, people have the power to be heard. Through social media, everyone has access to his own broadcast system. With the click of a mouse, your employees can tarnish your employer brand with evidence that lasts a lifetime. An employee's inappropriate behavior posted on a social media outlet can go viral, causing not only embarrassment but a potential lawsuit. All you have to do is search "Burger King Employee Taking Bath in Kitchen Sink," and more than five years after the incident there's still a digital footprint.

Leadership impact: Supervisors are the first line of defense in maintaining alignment on the front lines. Companies need to develop leaders at all levels within the company.

Transparency: We are all subject to Big Brother. Nothing is hidden. Privacy is a thing of the past. Transparency is now a given. Your company's bad customer service is likely to wind up on Twitter or Facebook for the world to see. The claim of sexual harassment against your executive may land as a headline on someone's blog.

Leadership impact: Companies must develop enlightened leaders who are aligned, aware, and accountable. The leader represents the company and guides employees back into alignment when they get off course. Without the proper character development and enough time for the new leader to shift his identity to embrace his new role, the leader will identify more with employees. As a result, the new leader will overlook inappropriate employee behaviors and fail to look out for the best interests of the company. In an instant, the bad behavior that the new leader was too afraid to address can cause damage that is not always easily repaired.

Choice: The ability to focus is almost a thing of the past. There's always something sparkling to get your attention. As a result, people are overwhelmed. Reports are late, tempers are short, and decisions are weak. The only relief is the distraction of social media, e-mail, or a sneaked-in game of Candy Crush. Simon Sinek, in his video, *Why Leaders Eat Last*, said that diagnoses for attention deficit hyperactivity disorders have increased by 66 percent in the last year. We have become addicted to the dopamine of distractions.[6]

Leadership impact: Enlightened leaders model responsible choice. They think about how their choices today affect operations tomorrow. When leading, they know how to manage their choices, and they "dial up" or "dial down" the choice factor to provide either freedom or structure, depending upon the intended result.

It's almost eerie to read what management consultant Peter Drucker predicted many years ago:

> In a few hundred years, when the history of our time is written from a long-term perspective, it is likely that the most important event those historians will see is not technology, not the Internet, not e-commerce. It is an unprecedented change in the human condition. For the first time—literally substantial and rapidly growing numbers of people have choices. For the first time, they will have to manage themselves. And society is unprepared for it.[7]

What Drucker predicted has already come to pass. The more choices we have, the lower our ability to self-manage. This inability to self-manage will have a huge impact on our companies if we do not develop enlightened leaders who light the way in our world of rapid change and uncertainty.

The reality that we live in is one of instantaneous change and extreme transparency. There is very little space between stimulus and response. People react out of emotion, without taking a pause to understand the bigger picture, and the potential power of our unconscious reactions. The problem is, there are no do-overs, and no place to hide. Even things you did in the past can come back to haunt you decades later. The best protection for the individual and for company leaders is to live an aligned, aware, and accountable life. That is why developing enlightened leaders will be viewed as a necessary investment in every organization that wants to thrive in these turbulent times.

Our world needs enlightened leaders at all levels: from the CEO to the supervisor, from the classroom to the boardroom. They are the ones who will promote culture change in our companies, communities, and classrooms. But first we must have the *will to be* enlightened leaders, *the eyes to see* what is possible, and the *power to create* the right environment for enlightened leaders to grow.

PART 1

The Will to Be

The final forming of a person's character lies in their own hands.

—Anne Frank

Mark's high-driving personality made him a high-earning sales star for his global pharmaceutical company. When he was promoted to district manager, he had the will to be a great leader. He knew everything about motivating his new sales team. After his first year, when Mark received the results from his team's evaluation of his leadership abilities, his first response was shock. His feelings then turned to anger. What worked for him as a salesman had not worked for him as a leader. At first Mark resisted the feedback. Then something changed.

The turning point was Mark's combination of *will* plus *willingness*. Will is about desire. Willingness is about the decision to do what is necessary. Desire without willingness equals an entitlement mentality. Willingness without desire is compliance.

A company can offer personality tests, assessments, training, and coaching, but all of these leadership development opportunities are useless unless the leader-to-be has the will to be and the willingness to do. Mark invited the team to his home for a private meeting where they had permission to "criticize to their heart's content," which they did.

The painful feedback gave Mark a new level of awareness. He learned that his methods of leadership did not align with team-work. Mark now realizes that leadership is a journey that takes alignment, awareness, and ongoing accountability. Mark regularly seeks feedback to keep himself accountable as he practices new relationship building and leadership skills. Today, his team loves him and always meets or surpasses its goals.

There is a place where resistance ceases and movement commences. I call this place the fulcrum point of change, meaning that when we are actively seeking change, there is a signature quality or state of "being" that is present right before the change. That state is willingness. Nothing happens until there is willingness.

I have learned that, no matter how great my coaching skills, I have absolutely no influence or power over someone who resorts to blame or who simply has no desire and no willingness to change. The same is true for companies that offer leadership development. If the leader doesn't desire growth and is not willing to learn, nothing happens.

The good news is that anyone who has the will to be a leader can make the decision to take charge of her own development. The desire to become a leader and the willingness to do what is required, whether or not the company provides the development, reflects the epitome of responsible aligned leadership. Blaming the company for not offering leadership development demonstrates an unenlightened perspective that feeds workplace drama. By contrast, you show an enlightened perspective when you make the decision to develop yourself.

The foundation for enlightened leadership is alignment, awareness, and accountability. Each requires the will to be, along with the willingness to do. In the next three chapters, you will begin to understand why alignment, awareness, and accountability are core qualities of enlightened leaders, and what happens when these qualities are missing.

CHAPTER 1

Aligned

There are only two ways to align: Tell yourself the truth or course correct.

—Marlene Chism

Misaligned values caused Bob Funk to leave the company where he had worked for seventeen years. "I would have worked there for the rest of my life," he said. "The owner was a fine man with strong principles. When he passed away, his son took over the company, and the culture changed."[1]

The new owner's values clashed so much with Funk's that he had no viable choice but to leave and start his own company, which he called Express Employment Professionals. Speaking of his decision to leave his former employer, Funk said, "The new owner, the president's son, was an accountant by trade, so the financial statements were the most important to him. What he didn't realize is that when you're in business, it's all about relationships, and good relationships build good financial statements."[2]

Today, Express Employment Professionals is the largest franchised staffing organization in North America, with over seven hundred franchises in the United States, Canada, and South Africa, employing more than 450,000 people in 2014. Thus, Funk's company is fulfilling his vision to help as many people as possible find good jobs by helping as many clients as possible find good people.

Many leaders have difficulty aligning the people and profit equation, and thus operate from an either-or mentality; however, Express Employment Professionals is a great example that shows how leading from alignment translates to business success. Since the end of the Great Recession in 2009, Express Employment Professionals achieved 152 percent growth, surpassing the staffing industry growth of 54 percent.

Although there are as many definitions for leadership as there are companies that have leaders, at the core, leadership is about alignment. Leaders leave companies when their personal values clash with the corporation's values. Leaders lose their jobs, their reputations, and sometimes even their freedom when their actions are misaligned with the law. Today's leaders can't get away with fooling the public as they might have in the past. The past decade has proven that their misalignment will eventually show up on the evening news or in social media.

The late Joe Paterno, former head coach of the Penn State football team, turned a blind eye to the fact that his assistant coach was sexually abusing players in the locker room. Paterno, considered one of the best coaches in history, was fired from Penn State, and the NCAA vacated all of his wins from 1998 through 2011 as punishment. When Paterno died in 2012, he left behind a stained legacy. John Edwards was at one time a top contender for the U.S. presidency until the public discovered he had fathered a child with one of his campaign workers. Bernie Madoff received the Congressional Medal of Honor for "unusual valor" in bringing hope to thousands. The world held him and his family in high esteem until it was discovered he had tricked investors by paying them their own money rather than profits. Lance Armstrong was considered one of the greatest athletes of all time until he finally admitted to taking performance-enhancing drugs to win races.

These examples of human beings who allowed themselves to move out of alignment have four things in common: they fooled the public; their actions eventually caught up with them; they experienced embarrassment and shame; and they hurt many innocent people, including their families.

What Is Alignment?

Merriam-Webster Dictionary defines "align" as "to arrange things so that they form a line or are in proper position; to change something so that it agrees with or matches something else."[3] When you buckle your seat belt, drive the speed limit, and use your signals properly, you are aligned with the law. When you drive under the influence of alcohol and ignore the speed limit, you are out of alignment with the law and with common sense.

Most people don't stop and think much about what alignment means. We *talk* about alignment a lot but haven't done much reflecting. Even less thought is given to being aligned with the mission and values of the company. My belief is that, because values live in the invisible realm of ideals, we tend to discount the importance of how behaviors and language either align or misalign with what we say we value.

If you say you value trust, then you must keep your commitments in order to stay aligned with that value. If you say you value kindness, then every time you are rude you are out of alignment with the value of kindness. If you say you value safety, then every time you consciously put yourself at risk, you are out of alignment with the value of safety. When you do something that is against your values, you are out of internal alignment. When you make a decision that does not match the mission and values stated on the company website, then you are out of alignment in your leadership. Integrity and alignment are identical twins.

Alignment is about making sure your walk matches your talk. Leaders who have thought seriously about their own values have a very good BS meter. They can tell immediately when someone is out of alignment. Those who have a strong internal alignment are not usually quick to believe everything they hear or see in the media, and they aren't prone to hero worship, whether that hero is a sports figure, a politician, or a business leader. Enlightened leaders have the eyes to see that everyone is subject to temptations that potentially diminish their integrity and take them out of alignment. That is why they value accountability, which we will talk more about in chapter 3. Enlightened leaders are quick to learn from the mistakes of misalignment.

The national news provides what I call a "drama perspective," focusing on the obstacle instead of the lesson. People love to talk about what everyone else is doing wrong. We view and then criticize high-profile leaders, sports figures, movie stars, and politicians who lose alignment with their constituents, with their family, or with the law of the land. Every single day people waste valuable time on social media arguing, debating, giving opinions, and making judgments while missing the point entirely.

Enlightened leaders understand the connection between personal and business integrity. Unenlightened people see a high-profile individual blatantly showing bad judgment, poor character, and misalignment in his personal life but conclude, "That is their personal life, and has nothing to do with business." Character is character, whether it's exhibited in business or in one's personal life. You cannot be misaligned in your personal life and be perfectly aligned in your leadership role. If leadership is about anything, it is about alignment.

Regardless of your definition of leadership, you won't achieve it without the will to align yourself to that definition. I had the privilege of interviewing one of the greatest leaders of our time, Frances Hesselbein, former CEO of Girl Scouts of the USA, and Presidential Medal of Freedom recipient. Hesselbein defines leadership as a matter of *how to be,* not *how to do*, saying, "We have spent half of our lives learning how to do, and teaching other people how to do. But we know in the end it is the quality and character of the leader that determines the performance—the results."[4]

The will to be aligned comes before alignment. If the will to be aligned is in place yet there is misalignment, the division is usually due to one or more of these three things: lack of awareness, lack of accountability, or competing values. We often see a clash of values when the drive to win at all costs takes over in sports, politics, or business.

Culture and the NFL

According to an October 2014 *USA Today* article, "Domestic Violence in Detail," NFL players have been investigated for more than fifty domestic violence cases under the leadership of Commissioner Roger Goodell.[5] The most prominent profiles of bad behavior to date include NFL star Ray Rice caught on video punching his fiancé; Chiefs linebacker Jovan Belcher killing his girlfriend, then committing suicide; and New York Jets linebacker Bryan Thomas punching his wife. No doubt a blind eye is often turned where sports are concerned. Perhaps it's difficult to align civil behavior with a sport that requires muscle, speed, and rough aggression to win, as football does.

The easiest out is to blame the top leader, Goodell, but the issue is much more complex, and belongs to all of us. As long as businesses promote the sport with their sponsorship dollars, and as long as football fans turn a blind eye and continue to watch the sport and buy tickets to the games, the problems will continue. As long as money, entertainment, and hero worship are the top values, nothing of substance is going to change. These are values issues, not policy issues. Policy is of no use unless the policy aligns with the corporate values.

What our society seems to value most is money and entertainment. As long as money is being made, there's not enough pressure to put a stop to the behavior. As long as people identify more with a team than they do with their own values, there's no reason for anything to change. This is a snapshot of how the values of the masses shape a culture. Businesses that sponsor the sport have the most leverage in influencing the behavior. Unfortunately, we often do not see the connection between that which we support and the values we claim. Each of us plays a role in what is tolerated, but until we become more enlightened, we will continue to look out of the window to see what everyone else is doing wrong instead of learning and leading from our own values.

Just as the official policies regarding behaviors that occur outside the NFL are overlooked, they are overlooked on the inside as well. When the Miami Dolphins suspended guard Richie Incognito in 2013 for bullying Jonathan Martin, who quit the team, the fallout included a legal investigation, a massive report, and millions in legal fees. As a result, the individuals involved suffered financially, but perhaps as important, they suffered emotionally. Incognito's cell phone text messages were made public, and both he and Martin suffered the emotional distress that comes with public exposure to private matters.

The locker-room culture of professional football is obviously different from corporate culture. Behavior and language that would never be tolerated in the average workplace are accepted and expected in the world of professional football. Bullying, hazing, harassment, and disrespect are part of the culture—and are downplayed as harmless fun—part of what it means to be a rookie, and so on. However, sports is still business, and there is much that companies can learn from studying alignment as it relates to both the world of sports and the world of business.

The first lesson is that policy that is not enforced doesn't matter. A policy that exists but is not enforced is a red flag of misalignment. These very same issues happen in all types of businesses every day.

The Miami Dolphins had a policy against harassment, bullying, and disrespect, but no one took the policy seriously. Most likely, none of the players even knew the policy existed. The policy and the reality of the culture were miles apart. To pretend the culture was anything but supportive of bullying is simply a matter of denying what is and has been true for decades—there is a lack of willingness to align with stated values.

Whether because of a lack of willingness or a lack of awareness, when the talk does not equal the walk, there is misalignment. We show our commitments not by the words we use but by the choices we make. When the marketing copy speaks about family values and respect, yet the living reality is about hazing, bullying, racial slurs, and emotional abuse, the light of media scrutiny will show a different commitment. Culture is not only about the inside environment, about a set of beliefs that govern behavior, or about "how we do things." Workplace culture also is influenced by the *outside* environment, which for the NFL includes sports fans, sponsors, and vendors.

In the end, as long as the organization's real commitment is aimed at maintaining the status quo—supporting a culture of misbehaving while talking about family values—problems and scandals will continue to surface. As long as fans continue to watch the sport and vendors continue to profit from the sport, the outside environment contributes to the problem.

There are only two ways to align: to tell the truth about your real values and to course-correct until your behaviors align with your values.

The Blind Eye

There is one truism that applies to any industry, organization, or workplace: you can't course-correct what you don't acknowledge. Whether it's due to blatant disregard, failure to acknowledge, or failure to speak up, the excuses are easy to spot—"I didn't know" or "I wasn't thinking." Turning a blind eye is not only about an unwillingness to see but a refusal to acknowledge a waving red flag.

Miami Dolphins head coach Joe Philbin ignored the fact that Incognito had a history of bullying, alcoholism, and anger management issues as far back as 2002, before he was hired to play for the Dolphins in 2010. According to USAToday.com, in the NFL, he quickly gained a reputation as a dirty player, and was even voted the league's dirtiest player in a 2009 survey by *Sporting News*.[6] Yet, when the abuse issues with Martin came to light, Philbin claimed he knew nothing about the abuse. Offensive line coach Jim Turner and head trainer Kevin O'Neill were fired not because they turned a blind eye but because they also participated in the abuse. There is a cultural aspect of Martin keeping the abuse to himself instead of speaking up, which I mentioned earlier. Most likely Martin was trying to avoid more harassment by teammates by staying silent and hoping the problem would go away. Maybe he thought he could just ride out the storm. However, Martin's inability or unwillingness to report the abuse caused him the very pain he was trying to escape by being silent: the incident became national news. It seems that either way, Martin was a victim and in a no-win situation.

In the end, it doesn't matter much if the blind eye is intentional or an oversight, the light of transparency will bring the darkness to light. More often than not, the misalignment is less dramatic, unintentional, and less visible, yet still causes a fair amount of drama. An example that comes to mind concerns an independent health-care organization I was consulting with, for a situation where the CEO was dissatisfied with the performance of a newly hired associate. Comparing the associate's written job description with the actual directions given to the employee, revealed that a misalignment had developed—a change in the company's direction had altered the needs of the role, but the description had not been updated and the change had not been communicated clearly to the associate.

Misalignment can be as simple as hiring an employee to do a job but then giving that person unrelated tasks that were not part of the initial job description.

Culture and Transparency

The cultures we are a part of influence our decisions and our beliefs. Each individual lives in many cultures, from general to specific: the culture of gender, the culture of country, the culture of the corporation, and the culture of *your* particular workplace. The culture of professional sports is vastly different from that of the average workplace. However, rather than looking at differences on the surface, we can learn from these examples in professional sports, in politics, and business. and look for patterns where the lessons are easy to discern. Once you spot the patterns, it's easier to recognize the more subtle patterns in your workplace or in your leadership.

When a company's policies support its stated mission, vision, and values, but its behaviors and decisions are out of sync, it's only a matter of time until the light of transparency exposes the deficit to the world.

Enlightened Leadership Is About Alignment

As a leader, you must assume the responsibility for maintaining alignment with the vision, mission, and values of your organization. The success or failure, and the ease or struggle, of your leadership journey depends upon alignment. Everything in your organization must align and work together. A job description needs to match the actual job being performed. The marketing material needs to truly represent what your company is about. The professionalism and demeanor of your people need to harmonize with the expectations of the industry in which you work. The language of the people in your organization needs to match the values posted on the website, and the talk in the halls needs to match the values posted on the walls.

Most of the time leaders do not realize how they contribute to drama. A highly skilled consultant or coach can be helpful because she will have the ability to see what cannot be seen by insiders. Sometimes we simply need someone else to turn on the light when we grope in the dark for the switch. In addition, leaders must be aligned with the rules of the game and the law of the land. Often overlooked is the reality that the leader must be aligned personally and spiritually, which we will talk about in a moment.

Signs of Misalignment

Your own discomfort or discontent—that inner knowledge that something is off—can alert you to a lack of alignment. It's common to believe the conflict is due to another person, situation, or circumstance. It's easy to take the drama perspective and complain about the company, the employees, the economy, or the weather. The enlightened perspective is to look inside to see what is out of alignment. Sometimes discomfort is a sign to speak up. At other times the discontent is a sign to move on. Sometimes it means you are not telling yourself the truth, or you have set unrealistic expectations. At other times, the discomfort indicates you are not living your values. To be fully aligned, you need to learn how to listen to your inner voice, to interpret your emotional landscape.

Scientists at the HeartMath Institute study how inner alignment impacts well-being. The mission of the Institute of HeartMath is to help establish heart-based living and global coherence by inspiring people to connect with the intelligence and guidance of their own hearts.[7] One term HeartMath uses is *coherence.* Coherence is a psychophysiological synchronization of your mental, emotional, and physical systems. The harmony of mind, emotion, and body working together is what I call spiritual alignment. Spiritual alignment is when your inner world is in harmony with your outer world. In short, your guidance comes from both the physical and nonphysical and from your relationship with self, others, and your higher power. Harry Emerson Fosdick, a prominent pastor in the early twentieth century said, "No man can be wrong with man and right with God." One of the biggest challenges we have with spiritual alignment in today's time is that we want to be only right with self. We often fail to consider others. We fail to consult with our higher power when making critical decisions. As a result we do not have the eyes to see the entire picture and how our choices affect others. We justify winning at any cost, as long as what we do aligns with our own personal values. We will talk more about how spiritual-awareness helps you to maintain spiritual-alignment in the following chapter.

We have a high regard for individuals who have a high degree of alignment in every sense of the word. While we admire them for making apparently difficult choices, from their perspective, they are just being authentic to who they are. Even their most difficult choices are enlightened and fully aligned with who they are. Their lives are aligned from the inner to the outer, and their decisions reflect self, others, and their higher power

Enlightened Choices

Enlightened choices come from aligning decisions with core values. One of my favorite thought leaders, social psychologist and neuroscientist Matthew Lieberman, was offered $3 million dollars to do research for eight months in Russia. The only catch was that he would have to be away from his wife and son. Lieberman turned down the offer, tempting as it was.[8] Perhaps at another time in his life he would have chosen to go to Russia. Values and priorities can shift depending upon our current situation, stage of life, and evolution. When you are in alignment with your values, you experience peace rather than cognitive dissonance, the conflict that comes from trying to hold incompatible beliefs simultaneously.

Neurosurgeon Zenko Hrynkiw demonstrated his clarity and alignment when he walked six miles through the 2014 Atlanta snowstorm to perform lifesaving brain surgery at Trinity Medical Center.[9] During the five-hour trek, he texted instructions to the surgical prep team. Rather than using the snowstorm as a reason to justify staying comfortable at home, Hrynkiw was led to act from a higher purpose—to do his job as a surgeon—and to save a life.

We are always amazed when we see individuals who live with such clarity and alignment, perhaps because most of us have never thought deeply about what we value, declared our values, then let those values be the guiding light for all the decisions we make. In the end, every person must be able to look in the mirror and respect the reflection. Those who are aligned, know themselves and they stay true to both their own values and to those of their company.

Declaring Values

A prerequisite to making enlightened choices is declaring your values. Until we *declare* our values, there is an accountability gap and no real alignment. There may be a plan or a vision, but getting to a desired result using any means possible is like cheating at Scrabble to claim the trophy. You may have won, but you know deep down that you wouldn't have if you had played by the rules. I believe that what fascinates the millions of viewers who watch the reality show *Survivor* is that the theme of the game is winning at any cost by outwitting, outsmarting, and outlasting the others. When a *Survivor* contestant tries to play by his own personal values of friendship, honesty, transparency, and fairness, rather than the game's values of outwitting, outsmarting, and outlasting, he always becomes disillusioned because he is eventually deceived, lied to, or blindsided by those playing according to the game's rules.

When a contestant struggles to align with the rules of the game and as a result sacrifices his sacred values of friendship, honesty, and trust, the contestant experiences cognitive dissonance. There is a psychological and spiritual discomfort that occurs when you operate outside your own values, whether you are aware of your values or not. The rude awakening comes when these contestants who are committed to playing by their *own* rules become upset when others play by the rules of the game—to outwit, outlast, and outsmart.

In business, you must be aware of the rules and values of the company you represent; otherwise, you will be disillusioned because you have failed to tell yourself the truth—that your values are not suited to the values of the company you work for. You can't win a game of *Survivor* by being honest, loyal, and telling the truth. Once values are declared, you create a new rule book of a higher order.

Yet, it's scary to declare a set of values. This is where we have to look in the mirror and become truly authentic about our weaknesses. When we decide to grow there is fear, possibly because the first experience is doubt and a feeling of being overwhelmed. We get to see the gap between where we are and where we say we want to be. Declaring values exposes a paradox: stating values sets you up for success, but to have that success, you have to look at where you have failed.

The reality is you have not failed. You can't fix what you don't acknowledge, and until you acknowledge and declare your values, you were not awake or aware. You must get over the fear of being "wrong" or falling into judgment. Spiritual leader and author of *The New Earth* and *The Power of Now* Eckhart Tolle says, "With the gift of awakening comes responsibility."[10] Once you are awake enough to declare your values, you have the responsibility to embody them, to take them as your own and to continue to make your decisions from the brightness of enlightenment rather than from the darkness of drama.

Competing Values

Misalignment, often experienced on a personal level, such as the lack of work–life balance, is due to competing values. As much as you value your family, you also value your career: being an excellent leader means sacrificing time with family. As much as you want to become physically fit, there aren't enough hours in the day for high-level personal care. The real problem is we don't know what the real problem is. We think the problem is about not having enough time. The real problem is lack of clarity about one's highest values.

As Peter Senge says in *The Fifth Discipline*, "The conflict between work and home is not just a conflict over time, but over values."[11] Unless you are clear about your values and declare them, you risk misalignment by succumbing to the temptations and thrills of the moment. When you are not aware of your values or when you are unaware of the priority of competing values, your desires compete for your attention and cause confusion. When we ignore our core values, or let competing desires take precedence over them, we veer off course.

When Lance Armstrong got caught using illegal performance-enhancing drugs to help him win in cycling, he was out of alignment

with the law and the rules of the game. He let his love of the lime-
light or perhaps the need to win at all costs override his will to play
by the rules. Even if one could argue that Armstrong was aligned
personally—say he valued winning whatever the cost, which neces-
sitated taking the drugs because everyone else did—he was still out
of alignment spiritually because he did not see the bigger picture
and how his decisions would create a giant ripple effect and negatively impact many others.

Indirectly, Armstrong's misalignment hurt many innocent people. Some might argue that he only hurt himself. The truth is that
more often than not, (with the game of Survivor being a possible
exception) you hurt others when you act out of alignment with the
rules of the game or the laws of the land. When Bradley Wiggins
won the Tour de France in 2012, Ben and Isabella, his two children, were bullied at grade school as their classmates accused their
dad of cheating.[12] He was associated with the sport of cycling and
indirectly associated with Armstrong, so Wiggins's win resulted in
schoolyard bullying and emotional drama for his children, which
was resolved only when Wiggins moved his kids to another school.
Whether we know it or not, our decisions and behaviors often have
a far-reaching ripple effect, even on those with whom we do not see
any immediate connection.

When Values Clash

Leaders lose perspective and balance when their personal values
clash with those of the organization they work for, causing cognitive dissonance and forcing them to choose between two equally
important values. The desire to fit into a culture that clashes with
your own values can obstruct your ability to lead. When forced
to choose between personal and corporate values, you risk your
career and suffer emotional trauma as you get chewed up by the
political system. In a nutshell, where values compete, there will

always be discomfort. The discomfort is the result of holding two or more important values that seem incongruent. Choosing or prioritizing one value over the other requires awareness and wisdom.

An unaligned leader can either stay silent or speak up. If the leader stays silent, he may experience stress-related illness, lowered productivity, anxiety, or any combination of these. If the leader decides to speak up or expose the misalignment, he risks loss of career, unwanted media attention, and potential financial loss. Either way, a leader is at risk when his values are at odds with the values of the company. (Later we will talk about how to use communication as a strategy when such instances occur so that risks can be minimized.) Noelle Roni, former principal of Peak to Peak Elementary School, a charter school in Lafayette, Colorado, personifies choosing personal values over corporate policy.

At Peak to Peak Elementary, it was policy for cafeteria workers to stamp the hands of schoolchildren whose accounts had no money in them, including those in the free lunch program. This policy created embarrassment for the kids in the program and for the children whose money had run out without being replenished. Roni decided this was inappropriate and demanded the cafeteria workers stop stamping hands for all children.[13] Drama erupted. When the food service manager resigned, a higher-up at the school demanded that Roni take responsibility for the resignation.

The power struggle between the principal and the administrator escalated, and when Roni refused to sign the documents and take responsibility for the resignation, she was fired. The community was outraged, and two board members faced a recall election, accused of creating an uncertain working environment. Upon further investigation, it was determined that the bylaws had been violated—the replacement of a principal required a public vote by the school's board. The failure to act with transparency tarnished the school's reputation while exposing the school to a potential lawsuit. The drama continued to unfold, with claims of a hostile work environment, a board that refused to disclose details, and parents groups that demanded the principal be reinstated. And all of the details were accessible to the public with a few mouse clicks or the push of a TV remote control button.

The Peak to Peak Elementary case offers insights into the complexities and issues involved when a leader's values conflict with those of the workplace. We see a disregard for due process, the impact of intense passion, and power struggles for authority, as well as decision making from many levels within the school, which are out of alignment with the mission and vision of the organization.

In our world of instant access to information, transparency occurs either as an enlightened choice to ensure accountability or as a response to drama. Transparency serves as either a preventive tool to create alignment or as a corrective tool after misalignment is exposed.

While we may not know all the issues surrounding this incident, one thing remains certain: transparency is no longer an option. It is a given. Any lack of alignment in our personal or professional lives may be broadcast for the world to see on national news platforms or via social media. This is why we need leaders who understand the principles of alignment and are willing to be aligned, aware, and accountable.

Executive Summary

- ➢ Alignment is when the walk equals the talk.
- ➢ Unenforced policies contribute to misalignment.
- ➢ When personal values clash with corporate values, misalignment results.
- ➢ Misalignment is often the result of competing values.

Wisdom Exercises

1. Describe a situation where you saw someone turning a blind eye.
2. Tell a friend or associate about an area where you often fail to speak up.
3. List the ways in which you model leadership by walking your talk.

CHAPTER 2

Aware

Empathy entails an act of self-awareness: We read other people by tuning in to ourselves.

—Daniel Goleman

Andrew, a middle-level manager of housekeeping at a rehabilitation center, was eager to become a leader, but his employees were difficult to manage. Andrew frequently got roped into games of verbal Ping-Pong with his employees.

"That's not fair."
"I didn't say it was fair."
"You didn't dock John's pay when he was late!"
"John has a better record than you..."
"I'm faster and get more done than John!"

Ping-Pong, Ping-Pong.

Employees constantly called in sick or made careless mistakes. Andrew's employees were willful and resistant to his leadership, and Andrew was resistant to the insubordination. He didn't want to terminate anyone because there was already a high degree of turnover, and letting an employee go meant not having someone to do the work.

Most executives seem unaware of the degree to which their supervisors' and managers' poor leadership skills are affecting employee absenteeism and turnover. For every complaint to Human Resources about bad boss behavior, there are another dozen instances not being reported. If there is significant turnover in a department as compared with the rest of the company, it's either the nature of the job or it's the leadership.

Andrew's frequent blowups were causing problems not only with his employees but with patients who occasionally witnessed his displays of emotion with his staff. Andrew shared his struggles with me during a coaching session.

"Something triggers me, and then I yell at my staff. I get so angry, I can't seem to control it."

"Is that the way you want to be?"

"No, that's not okay with me."

"Do you want to change?"

"I'm willing to change if you can teach me how."

"Absolutely, I can teach you how."

In the past, Andrew had blamed his employees for his outbursts, but now he was ready to turn his attention inward, to stop looking "out the window" to blame his employees and instead look "in the mirror" and take personal responsibility.

Awareness requires courage: the courage to look at what is difficult to see rather than avoiding, denying, or turning a blind eye. For enlightened leaders, awareness requires reflection and self-examination. You cannot be responsible unless you recognize choice, and you cannot recognize choice if you are not aware. Therefore, awareness from a leadership perspective always calls for responsible action: to course-correct when there is misalignment, to have difficult conversations, to make difficult decisions, and to choose between competing values to lead from integrity.

Without awareness we fail to realize that whatever is going on in our minds—the inner dialogue—eventually manifests into words and behaviors. The bloom on the flower is always attached to a root system. Awareness is that ability to reflect and recognize that behaviors are rooted in belief systems. Our inner dialogue eventually manifests into language, finally emerging as behavior. Awareness is always a prerequisite for alignment.

Obstacles to Awareness

Avoidance, procrastination, and excuse making indicate resistance—an unwillingness to be aware—which drives individuals to win at any cost. Leaders are willing to lose their souls to gain the world by allowing high performers to get away with inappropriate behaviors for the sake of profits. Leaders who aren't willing to be aware are destined to learn the hard way: they eventually experience the effect of misalignment. At some point, the discomfort they feel living out of sync with their values forces a willingness to become aware.

But here's the challenge for high-power leaders: the higher you rise in an organization, the less awareness you have of your own flaws. Daniel Goleman, author of *Focus: The Hidden Driver of Excellence*, says, "There's an intriguing relationship between self-awareness and power: There are relatively few gaps between one's own and others' ratings among lower-level employees. But the higher someone's position in an organization the bigger the gap. Self-awareness seems to diminish with promotions up the organization's ladder."[1]

In this chapter, we turn our attention to the will to be aware and the different forms of awareness.

Mike's Story

My client Mike, an equal partner in a family-owned business, struck me as educated, articulate, professional, and insightful. Other partners in the family business saw him differently. He constantly second-guessed himself and didn't speak up or share his ideas. His lack of courage filtered into his personal life. He avoided conflict with his wife, telling me, "I walk on eggshells, and I cringe when she calls my name." Mike knew something was out of alignment. He was stuck. "I still don't love my work, and I see no way to get out of the business. I don't have a plan, and I've invested way too much time and money to leave. I have decided to make a ten-year plan, and that should give me some clarity."

"Mike that is BS! Your plan will not work."

Now I had Mike's attention. Normally I like to use a candle or a flashlight, but it was clear to me that Mike needed a floodlight to wake him up.

"What?!"

"Until you get clear about what you stand for and how you want to show up in the world, you can't develop a plan or a road map that will ease the discomfort."

Values are like a compass. You can have a map, but if you don't know north from south you will have problems. Values are part of the strategy, not part of the tactics. Values tell you if you are going in the right direction, not what road to take to get there. Mike didn't know north from south, yet he was in the car backing out of the driveway.

"What are your top five values, Mike?"

"I don't know what my values are."

"Let's explore and experiment. Pick two to start with."

Mike was definitely stuck, so I decided, with Mike's permission, to take off the mentoring hat and put on the consulting hat.

"Mike, one of your values is courage."

"But I am not courageous in the least!"

"I know. That is why you are in discomfort. You have a value that you are not living."

This was truly an enlightening moment for Mike.

"Another value you have is grace."

"Yes! That is so true!"

Domains of Awareness

There are many types of awareness. Anytime you see someone who is extremely competent in an area, you could say she has a high level of awareness in that area. You can increase your awareness on virtually any topic or subject by simply studying and focusing on it for a period of time. Any area where you struggle is one where you have an opportunity to increase your awareness. The four major domains of awareness are:

- Self-awareness
- Other-awareness
- Cultural awareness
- Spiritual awareness

An enlightened leader is balanced in all four domains. Self-awareness is the ability to observe your own thoughts and emotions, likes and dislikes, and to know your own strengths and weaknesses. Other-awareness is the ability to read other people by listening to their voice inflections, watching their facial expressions, and observing their habits and mannerisms. Cultural awareness is the ability to observe the politics and structures that contribute to the culture. And spiritual awareness is the experience of universal principles and values. Let me share a story that illustrates the function of each domain in our lives.

Through self-awareness, Mike was able to identify his feelings.

He was able to observe his thought patterns and emotions, yet he was often more aware of others than he was of himself. This tendency contributed to problems in the family business and in his personal life. Mike was extremely aware of the politics of the company—after all, he was a partner—yet in many ways he was unaware of how the culture of his family business contributed to his emotional and cognitive dissonance. What amazed Mike was my ability to immediately identify two of his top values. You can observe someone's values by observing his life: What does he do? How does he talk? Where does he spend his time and money?

Mike's dilemma was how to turn his conflicting values into congruent values. He had a soft answer even in the midst of drama, but sometimes his desire to embody graciousness conflicted with his need to show courage, speak his truth, and have difficult conversations.

A drama perspective could drive Mike to view his business partners as the obstacle and to view his wife as unreasonable. A more enlightened perspective would enable him to see these individuals as teachers who could help him develop one of his highest values: courage.

Until you declare your values, you may remain unaware of what they are. Anytime you have cognitive dissonance that comes from not being true to yourself, you may have a spiritual awareness issue, one of not knowing how to align competing values so all are balanced and congruent.

Spiritual Awareness

According to Deepak Chopra, physician, author, and world-renowned expert in the field of mind–body healing, the domain of spiritual awareness involves experiencing universal values. Spiritual awareness is not about religion but about experiencing joy, compassion, purpose, insight, truth, and beauty. I like to think of spiritual awareness as a direct connection with the Divine, a higher power that acts as a navigational system that alerts you when you are getting off course. This inner connection supplies you with the ability to self-correct, to find the part of yourself that is in charge, even if it seems you are at the mercy of your feelings, thoughts, or circumstances. This awareness is available to every human being who is willing to take full responsibility for her inner life and outer life. Spiritual awareness helps us to maintain spiritual alignment. Spiritual alignment is when we are in harmony with self, others, and our higher power. If any one of these are out of balance, there will be a spiritual-awareness deficit.

Mike was a generous and gracious individual. He always saw the good in people. He was a religious person with a strong faith, yet his awareness issue was a spiritual one because in trying to appease others he became alienated from himself, and he did not see any way out of his situation. He was often overcome with the feeling that there was no escape, as his mind swirled with worry and anxiety. I recognized Mike's dilemma as a spiritual-awareness issue. He had lost the part that was in charge.

I asked Mike to declare his values, but he was afraid to do so: "What if I'm wrong, and what if the values I pick aren't the truth? What do I do then?"

"You get to change them! You are the creator of your experience."

That's when I shared a concept I call *trying on your values*.

Trying On Values

The awareness and declaration of a value requires that you embody it. This is why there is often a resistance to declaring values, an example of being unwilling to become aware. The fear usually arises because we don't know what will be required to embody a particular value. For example, if you say that respect is a value, what will that require of you? It may require you to work on being more patient. You may be required to stop interrupting, rolling your eyes, or hanging up on telemarketers. You must combine the will to be with the willingness to do.

It takes great courage to get real about your true values, so I suggest you and your fellow leaders "try on" a value for a week or two before you commit to it. Think of trying on values as you would think of shopping on approval. When you go into a high-end clothing store, you see an expensive coat, but the price on the tag seems a bit out of range. The shop owner says, "Why don't you take it home on approval and wear it around the house. Take it out one night and see how it feels. If you like it, take off the tag and call us, and we'll charge it to your account."

Similarly, every value you try on has a price tag. When you own the value, you take off the tag, and you are *willing* to pay the price. For example, if you value courage, the price is a willingness to have difficult conversations. If you value health, the price is the discipline it takes to eat well and exercise. If you value compassion, the price is limiting your temptation to judge harshly.

If the Value Fits, Wear It

How do you know if your declared values fit? You know by the way you feel when you try them on and by what you see when you look in the mirror. Do the values fit you, or are they too big? Can you grow into them or have them altered to fit you so that you are in alignment? Are you willing to reprogram old habits that do not support the value? Are you willing to pay the price to wear the values? In other words, are you willing to marry your vision to your values even when it may be easier in the short term not to do so? There are only two ways to align: either change your behavior to match your value, or change your value to match what you are already doing.

Alignment itself is a spiritual principle. To be aligned is to be complete and whole, lacking nothing: it is to be undivided and to have integrity. Spiritual awareness helps you to stay aligned so that your walk matches your talk. Spiritual awareness helps you know when it's time to course-correct. You cannot really know your values unless they are tested. By your choices, you reveal your commitments.

The same parallel can be found in the biblical faith-versus-works argument: "Show me your faith without your works and I will show you my faith by my works."[2] When we know our values (personal or company) but have not declared them as our own and internalized them, we experience confusion and inconsistency. Spiritual awareness is the highest level of awareness and influences all other domains of awareness. When your personal values conflict internally, you will inevitably send mixed messages to your clients and employees, who will perceive your lack of authenticity.

Self-Awareness

Self-awareness is a prerequisite for personal and leadership growth. Self-awareness helps you to understand your thoughts and emotions and how they combine to create stories, meaning, and interpretation. Understanding your emotions helps you to know when you are irritated so that you learn how to speak up or set a boundary. Let's go back to the story of Andrew, the manager of housekeeping at the rehab center. Andrew had learned how to stuff his emotions, which resulted in frequent blowups. Andrew thought he had an anger problem, but in reality he had a self-awareness problem. Once Andrew learns how to notice the triggers before he reaches a boiling point, and he learns and practices the communication skills he needs to gain cooperation from his staff, he will actually modify the neuro-connections in his brain. At the same time, he will have more confidence and greater competence, and he will be able to influence the people he leads.

Self-awareness is imperative for you to accurately interpret your emotions. Unaware people tend to blame others or make excuses, because that's the path of least resistance. Self-awareness is the ability to observe the thinking mind. We think more than sixty thousand thoughts per day, and 85 percent of them are either negative or repetitive.[3] Most of us are not aware of how much our inner dialogue affects our performance and leadership effectiveness. We all operate from our belief systems. Some of our beliefs work for us, and some are dysfunctional—consider Mike's belief that he should never disagree with his wife or his business partners. As a leader, your dysfunctional beliefs affect your workplace culture as well as your own health and well-being.

A few years ago, I interviewed Dr. David Simon, a neurosurgeon who was Dr. Deepak Chopra's business partner. Dr. Simon said that negative core beliefs contribute to illness: "We know now there is an intimate relationship to the mind and body."[4] Self-awareness includes the ability to notice and monitor your thoughts and to accurately label your feelings. Dr. Simon said, "Our immune cells are eavesdropping on our internal dialogue."[5] You are constantly sending messages to your immune system.

A lack of awareness about your inner dialogue affects both your personal health and the health of your organization. Self-awareness helps you gain the wisdom of discernment, promotes personal responsibility, and is a prerequisite for effective leadership.

Leadership impact of self-awareness: it is impossible to be a critical thinker if you believe everything you think or if you let your emotions run the show. If you consistently refuse to become aware of your feelings or avoid telling yourself the truth, your deceptiveness will leak into your leadership role. Increasing your self-awareness increases confidence and competence while elevating your executive presence.

Other-Awareness

Other-awareness allows you to tap into and empathize with what others are going through, without taking on their feelings. It is the ability to listen intently and see what is possible for the other without judgment. Many times leaders have either an overabundance or a deficiency of other-awareness.

Leaders who have an overabundance of other-awareness live out of integrity with their own values much of the time. They do things they don't agree with to keep the peace, as Mike often did to appease his business partners. The telltale sign of having too much other-awareness is taking on other people's issues. You can recognize these leaders by the way they avoid difficult conversations. Sometimes they fear hurting others' feelings, or they tell employees what they want to hear to keep the peace. Another habit is listening to employees' gossip about other employees. Employees may like these kinds of leaders, but they won't respect them. They often perceive this type of leader as soft or inauthentic even if they are unable to articulate it. Mike's failure to identify his values while walking on eggshells around his business partners and his wife shows what can happen when you let other-awareness overshadow your awareness in the other domains.

On the other hand, leaders who are low on other-awareness or who don't care how their employees feel contribute to a culture of mistrust. Employees are guarded in the presence of this type of leader and often perceive the leader as self-absorbed, arrogant, or lacking in empathy. Or, as in Andrew's case, employees believe that the leader who has outbursts does not care for them, so they in turn do not care for the leader.

Justifying rude behavior in the name of "honesty" while blaming employees for being too sensitive indicates an others-awareness deficiency. Another sign is the inability to listen or consider another point of view. If there is turnover in a particular department, as there was in Andrew's department, investigate to see whether you have a leader who is insensitive to the way other people feel. This type of leader does not know how to motivate people, gain their trust, or build a collaborative environment.

One of my blog readers living in China shared this with me in an e-mail:

> As an English teacher in a five-star hotel in China, I find it fascinating when staff comes to class so eager to speak and engage and then return to their jobs terrified and stoic. Managers tell me all the time that their English needs help, but I often wonder if they are just terrified to make mistakes around their manager? What's the cost of being an intimidating leader? Do people leave jobs or do they leave managers?[6]

Human beings are either in growth mode or protection mode. Negative feedback, when it is delivered in an emotional or thoughtless manner, poses a threat to the brain of the person receiving the feedback. When the brain receives a threat, the limbic system stimulates the fight or flight response, and the other person goes right into protection mode. The part of the brain responsible for learning (the neocortex) shuts down so that the energy can be better spent protecting oneself.

Leadership impact of other-awareness: leaders who combine high self-awareness with high other-awareness are able to increase performance and gain cooperation without manipulation. Self-absorbed leaders fail to notice how their behaviors affect others. They look out of the window instead of in the mirror, missing the signs that indicate a lack of leadership ability. Instead, they judge employees as weak while missing the possibility that perhaps they themselves are the weakest link. Leaders who justify disrespectful communication, abrupt feedback, or emotional outbursts contribute to avoidable workplace drama. The dilemma may not even be noticed until the more visible signs of drama emerge: turnover, absenteeism, and low morale.

Cultural Awareness

Leaders need to grow in their awareness of their organization's culture. If you are not aware of how things work, the rules of the game, and the politics and structure of your work environment, you will continue to be surprised, stressed, stirred up, or even embarrassed by the "global issues" that affect your work world.

One of my colleagues, writer and consultant Tim Boden, worked for almost two years in China. Tim said, "Major management techniques over there include browbeating, intimidation, and embarrassing employees in front of their peers. It's considered perfectly acceptable."[7] In his experience, employees who work for a manager who uses Western management principles think the manager is weak, and they try to take advantage of the stupid foreigner.

In most prisons, the culture includes a "code of silence" among inmates, who agree that even if you are beaten or stabbed, you keep quiet. Perhaps one reason Miami Dolphins lineman Jonathan Martin did not speak up about the bullying and harassment he experienced is because he had a high level of awareness of a similar culture in professional football. Speaking out would have been political suicide. Much of the time a lack of cultural-awareness simply leads to a mild hand slapping, some confusion, or embarrassment.

Leadership impact of cultural awareness: you must know the rules of the game and understand the dynamics and politics in an organization, or your decisions will not be wise and your communication will be reactive rather than strategic. Study the culture. Learn the rules of the game. Know how it works before you try to initiate any changes.

Clarity Versus Awareness

I want to make a distinction between clarity and awareness. Clarity is about knowing what you want. Any area where there is drama is always an area where there is either a lack of clarity or a lack of awareness. You can be clear about what you want but still unaware of how your habits or behaviors keep you from getting what you want. On a personal level, you may be clear about your desire to have a successful marriage yet be unaware of how your resentment is keeping you from success. Mike was clear he wanted to be happy, but he was unaware his habit of not telling others his truth actually contributed to his feeling of unhappiness.

Awareness is about a deeper knowledge that includes the four domains, self, other, cultural, and spiritual. Clarity combined with awareness can change any situation. Figure 2-1 illustrates this principle, showing in succession starting from left to right, high clarity and low awareness; low clarity and high awareness; and finally both high clarity and high awareness.

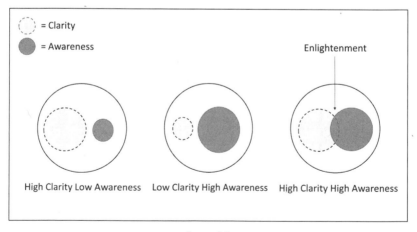

Figure 2-1

As a leader, you may be clear about the type of team you want to develop but unaware of how your leadership skills prevent you from developing that team. You may be clear about the rules of the game but unaware of the workplace politics and nuances in the corporate culture. If you are clear about what you want yet you continue to struggle, then I guarantee you have a lack of awareness on some level. As I said, someone may be clear yet unaware, as shown in the first illustration on the left of figure 2-1.

Now looking at the middle circle (Low Clarity, High Awareness) you see an example of someone who may have a high level of awareness in all or any of the domains, yet is not clear about her objectives.

Finally, when there is a high degree of both clarity and awareness so that they overlap, there is enlightenment as you can see in the last illustration on the right. Enlightenment is when you have enough clarity and awareness to make the best decisions that align with your values, the company's values, and the bigger picture.

Discomfort, unhappiness, or any type of drama is a signal that you should pay attention and to potentially course-correct. Paying attention to thoughts and emotions helps clarify desires. For example, interpreting anger as a sign that a boundary has been crossed or as indication that you should speak up and be more direct is a more accurate and helpful interpretation than construing your anger to mean someone is purposefully trying to stand in your way. When you interpret frustration as a sign that you need to ask for help or need to take a break, you learn how to better manage your own stress while gaining the cooperation of others. In this way, enlightened leaders can use drama to sharpen clarity and awareness.

When you are connected to your truth, you have the ability to discern truth in others. For example, when you hear an employee complaining, instead of labeling him a troublemaker, you may realize the employee doesn't have the skills to communicate effectively or the confidence to initiate the needed change. Enlightened leaders do their own inner work and, as a result, know that others also have the capacity to change.

When you listen carefully without judging, advising, or interrupting, you increase your awareness of others. When you pay attention to your corporate culture—the nuances, the relationships, the structures, and the patterns—you elevate your cultural awareness. When you notice incongruities between the company's vision, mission, and values and the behavior of those acting on behalf of the company, you become more discerning and begin recognizing lack of alignment.

Spiritual awareness helps you to experience the joy of leading from a higher purpose in alignment with your declared values and with the values of the corporation. Balancing awareness in all four domains helps you lay a foundation for a culture of accountability.

Executive Summary

➤ Four domains of awareness are self, other, cultural, and spiritual.
➤ Human beings are either in growth mode or protection mode.
➤ Declaring values increases awareness.
➤ When you are connected to your truth, you can discern truth in others.

Wisdom Exercises

1. Consider the area of awareness you need to develop, or discuss the matter with a colleague.
2. Make a list of your top four values, and then *try them on*.
3. Ask someone you trust what she sees as your blind spot.

CHAPTER 3

Accountable

A body of men holding themselves accountable to nobody ought not to be trusted by anybody.

—Thomas Paine

A s Jackie waited for the lawyers to discuss the results of the settlement, she reflected on the yearlong process of terminating a disruptive employee. Jackie, the senior human resources director for a regional medical center, swore she would leave the company the next time she saw similar red flags. The employee she'd let go had more than twenty years of service at the medical center. The nurse was considered a high performer, so her behavior had been tolerated as each supervisor avoided the difficult conversation. "It has been a painful process, as this employee had been tolerated for eighteen years, occasionally talked to, but because she was considered a high performer she was allowed to carry on, hurting patients, families, and staff along the way as well as creating chaos in her wake of disruption," Jackie recalled.[1]

The process took a toll on Jackie and her team. "Addressing a high performer is very difficult. One thing I have found myself saying is that I would never do this again. I would move away or change jobs, as it has been very negative and unpleasant. I didn't realize how hard it would be emotionally and mentally," she said.[2]

Responsibility and Accountability

The difficult conversations avoided today become the lawsuit the company fights a decade later. Every single day, supervisors and managers complain about employees' behavior and lack of accountability, but ultimately the problem is the leader's lack of responsibility, evidence of which is the evasion of difficult conversations.

Unenlightened leaders move the employee to another department, location, or cubicle, while the roots of the drama continue to spread. If leaders are unwilling to take ownership, how can those same leaders blame the employee? Signs that indicate a lack of leadership include:

- Blaming employees instead of coaching them
- Avoiding performance feedback
- Gossiping about the employee's ineffectiveness
- Transferring the troublemaker to another department
- Firing a long-term employee who has had no warning
- Making excuses for the lack of clear direction
- Failing to communicate expectations

There are many reasons individual leaders struggle with responsibility and accountability. Here are four of the main ones:

1. They do not understand the distinction between responsibility and accountability.
2. They do not have appropriate support or resources.
3. They have a skills gap.
4. They lack discipline.

Failing to understand the distinction between being responsible and being accountable is a chief reason leaders struggle. Responsibility comes from the heart and accountability from the head. You *accept* responsibility, but accountability (to superiors, stockholders, and perhaps the public) can in a sense be forced on you. We talk about being *held* accountable, which suggests punishment, blame, and shame.

The second reason some people resist accountability is that they have not had the proper support or resources. When someone has responsibility for a job and is measured on his effectiveness, he will avoid accountability if he is not confident he can accomplish the job. The right support and resources fixes this problem.

The third reason leaders sometimes avoid accountability is a skills gap. They may be disorganized, not know how to delegate, or simply may not be critical thinkers. I've seen even high-level leaders who did not get back to people, dropped balls, and made promises that were not fulfilled unless they were reminded again and again. These patterns indicate a potential problem with accountability because the leaders do not have the right skill set.

The fourth problem is discipline. Sometimes leaders have too much power, and because no one seems to be holding *them* accountable, they lose awareness that their own lack of discipline sets a bad example.

The more these kinds of problems are tolerated, the more poor decisions affect the culture. The only reason an employee is disruptive, lazy, confrontational, or ineffective is because it is allowed. When a leader has a drama perspective, she blames the employee. Initially, blaming feels better than taking responsibility. As long as the problem is Ron, Rick, or Randy's performance, there's no personal development and no personal responsibility required on the part of the leader.

A leader with a more enlightened approach asks, "What can this employee teach me about my leadership weaknesses?" These kinds of questions are never asked until you shift your identity from supervisor to leader. Companies that consciously decide to develop leadership identity have much more success with creating a culture of accountability.

Leadership Identity and Accountability

I had the opportunity to interview Joe Chinn, assistant city manager, and Stacey Peterson, the chief people officer for the City of Rancho Cordova in California. Peterson said, "One of our core values is leadership—every employee has a leadership role."[3] Rancho Cordova was the first government agency to make the 50 Best Small and Medium Workplaces List put out by Great Place to Work. If an employee at Rancho Cordova sees that a coworker needs additional training or assistance, he steps up as a leader and offers ways to be supportive or collaborative. Coworkers who see a colleague failing to deliver the best possible customer service are encouraged to share ideas. Or they can coach coworkers on various ways to support and serve their customers so that the positive experiences from customers turn into positive stories that filter out into the community. This is just one example of how accountability becomes a way of life when everyone identifies as a leader.

More formal methods also are applied at Rancho Cordova. Employees get ongoing feedback through a performance management system as well as feedback from managers or supervisors. This program is designed to reinforce leadership qualities as employees exhibit them and to point out where there might be additional opportunities to grow their leadership abilities.

A lack of accountability in the workplace can be as small as the leader avoiding difficult conversations or as big as the corporate scandals that make headlines in the national news. In the world of big business, companies lose millions and billions of dollars each year due to lack of accountability. With a few clicks of a mouse, you can read the CliffsNotes version of corporate scandals dating from the fifteenth century through today, and from all around the world.[4]

Accountability Versus Responsibility

The words *responsibility* and *accountability* are used interchangeably as defined in the dictionary. However making a distinction between responsibility and accountability enables leaders to promote enlightened accountability. The distinction I make is this: Responsibility is about owning or taking on an obligation. Accountability is about measuring and reporting how well you fulfilled that obligation. The act of measuring (accountability) is intended to increase a sense of ownership (responsibility).[5]

However if you look at any situation where someone was skewing the numbers, or reporting false information, it is because there was no real ownership (responsibility) to begin with. Misalignment occurred because looking good became more important than telling the truth in order to course-correct.

Enlightened leaders know that if responsibility comes first, accountability simply helps keep people on track with their commitments. The distinction is powerful: when employees take ownership first and have adequate support, accountability is welcomed. When people don't take ownership, they devise ways to avoid accountability.

When accountability is used to force responsibility, people may purposely skew the numbers, hide information, or avoid seeking the truth. Start talking about accountability, and you will notice that people tense up. It doesn't have to be this way.

Responsibility Comes First

I became even more convinced that responsibility must come before accountability after talking with John Reynolds, vice president of business development for the International Franchise Association. He said:

> One of the reasons that franchising is such a cool business model is because of the principle of ownership. The

franchisor is not only looking for financial capital, they are looking for emotional capital, intellectual capital. Therefore, when a franchisee buys into that franchise, they are buying into the brand of the company. The franchisee is bringing passion and emotional capital to the table, which is priceless. That is not something that the franchisor can buy.[6]

Reynolds explained that franchises work because, instead of hiring fifty managers, a franchisor gets fifty owners. "Unless that general manager has some stake in the business through **ownership,** then they're not likely to be as motivated or as passionate about the business. When you own something, you invest in it mentally and emotionally in a way that you don't when you don't own something," he said. [7]

Many people will avoid accountability if they have not taken ownership. Financial ownership aside, passion born out of mental and emotional ownership is necessary before accountability has any power.

What is the link that makes someone embrace accountability? It is the passion she brings to achieve her vision. "Whether you are a Wall Street broker, or the guy that drives the local pizza delivery truck, if you are not invested in it mentally, and psychologically, you won't get satisfaction from your job," Reynolds said.[8] Passion induces individuals to take full ownership—responsibility for the outcome. People who are invested in some way welcome accountability. In fact, with the right mind-set and the right support within the culture, accountability can be mentally stimulating, rewarding, and even fun.

Modeling Accountability

If ever there was a role model for accountability as fun, it is CEO Lauren Dixon. As head of Dixon Schwabl, a full-service advertising agency in Rochester, New York, Dixon exemplifies leadership that is aligned, aware, and accountable. In June 2010, *Inc.* magazine ranked Dixon Schwabl as one of the top twenty small company workplaces in America and the firm has been selected as one of the Great Place to Work Best Small Workplaces in America list. Dixon models accountability perfectly by voluntarily making herself answerable to those "under" her. Normally, a person senses the obligation to his bosses, but great leaders consciously make themselves accountable to subordinates as well.

Every year Dixon has her eighty-five team members take the Great Places to Work survey so she can see how her team rates the company. "Until you do the survey you don't really know—you're guessing. You may think you have a great culture but the nuggets of information that a company can get from going through the survey and the process are golden,"[9] she said.

Dixon models both responsibility and accountability. As CEO, she takes responsibility (ownership) for consciously creating a workplace culture that aligns with the core values of the business. She shows accountability by looking at data directly from her employees to help her understand the perceptions of employees and to discern where there is area for improvement. "It's Christmas for me. As soon as I get that report, I lock myself in my office and I pore over the data because I always learn something. I learn what we're doing really well, but more importantly I learn of the work that we need to focus on in the coming year,"[10] she said.

Alignment Versus Accountability

Alignment is first, accountability second. In other words, you may be able to reach a goal at any cost, but when you move toward a goal while maintaining alignment with your values, winning is more narrowly defined. For example, the five core values of Dixon Schwabl are respect, integrity, teamwork, giving back to the community, and fun. For Dixon Schwabl, every decision is made within the framework of its five core values.

While alignment is about congruence, accountability is about the *evidence* of congruence, and ultimately about the course corrections along the way that allow a company to align with its values while reaching its goals. In fact, course correction is such an important component of accountability that I have dedicated an entire chapter to the concept in the next section. Dixon told me that when someone doesn't share the values instituted at Dixon Schwabl or when there is evidence a team member is speaking disparagingly about another, the leadership team takes quick action to make the needed course correction.

When the leader truly embodies company values, the team follows suit. "What I love about my team here is they are such ambassadors of our culture that they call individuals out even before I witness it. They'll pull a team member to the side and say, 'Hey, that type of behavior might've been tolerated at your previous company but we don't do that here.' That person has a chance to change their wicked ways," [11] Dixon added.

Identifying Absence of Responsibility

If a leader experiences problems in her business or in a particular department, the problem may be more about responsibility than accountability. Responsibility is about the commitment: the ownership of the task, project, or job.

The way to identify problems related to responsibility in an employee is to listen for these phrases:

- "That's what everyone else was doing."
- "I was just following orders."
- "I thought it didn't really matter."
- "It's not my job."

- "I forgot."
- "I didn't know...."
- "It was just too difficult."

As you can see from the snapshot above, the language that indicates a lack of responsibility is full of complaints, excuses, and regrets. Individuals who take ownership use responsible language. Accountability will be little more than a whipping stick if there is no development of a responsible mind-set. When an owner or high-level leader does not have a responsible mind-set, you will always see these components: a lack of awareness, a lack of clarity, and irresponsible language. Let me share a blueprint of a conversation I have with managers that happens all too often:

"I have an employee who is almost useless."

"What is he doing that he should not be doing?"

"It's hard to pinpoint."

"Well, what should he be doing that he is not doing?"

"It's not one thing in particular—it's more of an attitude."

"How long has he been with you?"

"For over ten years."

"Well, he must have been a good employee at one time. What changed?"

"You make a lot of assumptions." [Said in a defensive tone.]

"When was the last time you talked with him about his behavior?"

I could go on and on with this dialogue, and it goes nowhere. First, the leader is not clear about what needs to happen, and is unaware of his own blind spots. Second, the problem has gone on way too long. Third, the leader blames the employee even though the leader has the authority to get coaching for the employee, investigate cause, or even fire her. The language is full of blame and avoidance. Until the leader is willing to own the responsibility for the success of the company or department, "accountability" is just another way to cast judgment and find blame. Leaders need to pay attention to their language to make sure they are speaking from clarity, responsibility, and accountability, before pointing fingers at employees for ineffective performance.

Responsibility Is the Bridge

Responsibility is the bridge between alignment and accountability. Leaders who want to promote a culture of accountability have to first take responsibility for creating that kind of culture. **A blaming mind-set from the leader cannot produce a culture of accountability among employees.** Once the leader has a mind-set of embracing responsibility, she will find it easy to notice when employees avoid responsibility. Without a responsible mind-set, accountability becomes something to avoid—a judge instead of a witness. When the leader or manager who is holding others accountable offers mentoring rather than judgment, it's relatively easy to help employees make the shift.

In any area where you see a problem, you can bet that taking full responsibility could solve that problem. You might find that it's a leader, an associate, or an employee (or all three!) who is avoiding responsibility. Leaders must take full responsibility for their own emotions, for the business results, and for the culture in which they lead. If a leader has emotional outbursts and blames employees, this behavior must be corrected. If a leader complains about others not being accountable, self-examination may be in order.

Getting the right support for an outcome or a project makes responsibility feasible and accountability a friend instead of a foe. Here is a huge distinction that will help you examine your own level of personal responsibility and examine the level of responsibility of your teammates, associates, or employees: those who are **willing to be responsible** use accountability as information to tell them when they are on or off course, and they see the person to whom they report as a witness. In contrast, those who **avoid** responsibility have learned to fear accountability because they interpret the person to whom they report as a judge. Work on the relationship between the one reporting and one being reported to, and see if an improved dynamic between the two shifts the resistance to accountability.

Clarity and Accountability

When a leader is responsible and supports the supervisors who report to her, accountability is simply a light that illuminates the current reality as measured against the desired outcome. So, when a leader complains and I ask the question, "What is he (the employee) doing that he should not be doing?" and the answer is, "I don't know" or "It's hard to say," that tells me there is a lack of clarity.

The one component always present in drama is a lack of clarity. Let me make a distinction: just because you are not clear does not mean you are creating drama, but I promise that wherever there is drama there is a lack of clarity.

The most difficult question for people to answer is usually, "What do you want?" When there is a lack of clarity you will hear complaining about what is not happening, or you will hear excuses, stories about the past, and other forms of distraction. To clearly answer the question, "What do you want?" you must define a desired result. Evidence of clarity is the ability to articulate, in one paragraph or less, the intended result. This is true even when speaking about the minutest details of poor employee performance.

For example, to say that Janet has a bad attitude is to make an assumption. To say that Janet slammed down the phone, raised her voice, and then rolled her eyes is to articulate an observable set of behaviors, which brings about clarity. This observation details what she is doing that she should not be doing: slamming down the phone and rolling her eyes. From that, it is possible to define what Janet should be doing that she is **not doing**: asking for help and taking a break when she gets stressed. When the leader gains clarity, then she can communicate with the employee to express the exact changes needed to improve performance. Until then, expect a fair amount of drama.

Why People Fear Accountability

The word accountability elicits a threat response for most people. Any time there's a disaster, mistake, or misfortune on the news, the first thing out of the mouths of officials is, "Who is to be held accountable?" The tone is always one of shame and blame, and fingers start to point before facts are given. What is not taken into consideration is that a responsible mind-set and accountability throughout a process often means that there won't be a need to "hold someone accountable." Real accountability helps you to see molehills before they become mountains. Enlightened accountability is simply a process of checking in with reality, measuring it against the stated goal, reporting to the appropriate individual, and making course corrections as needed along the way. People fear accountability, however, because they view it as persecution instead of as protection.

People experience fear when they don't feel in control. Three things lead people to feel a sense of control: resources, knowledge, and mind-set. If the mind-set is about learning, and if the knowledge and resources to meet the goal are available, accountability is a breeze.

Here is a formula to overcoming fear: Knowledge + Resources > Fear. How would you feel if your computer broke down during a big project? Your experience would be different depending upon the combination of your mind-set, your knowledge, and your resources. If you had a background in IT or if your company provided a technician and a new computer while yours was in the shop, at the most you would be inconvenienced. If you are a freelance writer on a deadline and don't know anything about computers, and you don't have the money to fix the computer, your experience would be dramatically different. Understanding the importance of knowledge and resources is the easy part. Now let's look at the importance of mind-set.

Mind-Set

In her fascinating book *Mindset: The New Psychology of Success*, Carol Dweck makes the distinction between a growth mind-set and a fixed mind-set. As one of the world's leading researchers in the fields of personality, social psychology, and developmental psychology, Dweck says those who have a growth mind-set believe they can *develop* themselves; therefore, they are open to accurate information about their current abilities even if it's unflattering. Those who have a fixed mind-set believe that intelligence and ability are carved in stone; therefore, their fixed mind-set creates an urgency to prove themselves over and over. Dweck says, "When you enter a mind-set, you enter a new world. In one world—the world of fixed traits—success is about proving you're smart or talented. Validating yourself. In the other—the world of changing qualities—it's about stretching yourself to learn something new. Developing yourself."[12]

Can you see the impact a fixed mind-set might have on accepting or avoiding accountability? Think about a leader who has a growth mind-set trying to coach an employee with a fixed mind-set. The capacity for drama is high when you combine a fixed mind-set with scores for performance. I believe this is why people cheat or avoid looking at the data—they are afraid to see where they need to improve. The fear is based on the belief that the assessments will reveal that they need to improve in ways that their intelligence or abilities won't permit. The next reaction is self-judgment. Self-judgment is a by-product of a fixed mind-set.

When you have a growth mind-set, you look at accountability

measures as needed information to help you make the necessary corrections that will help you achieve your goals—as Lauren Dixon does when looking at survey results from her employees. The data simply tells her what is working and what is not working from her employees' view. Dixon is excited to get the survey because she is not afraid of the information. "If you can crack the code, it's such an incredible feeling. It really is, and I always look forward to getting the information because it's such rich data," she said.[13]

The distinction between those who make friends with accountability and those who don't has to do with a growth mind-set versus a fixed mind-set as well as the ability to take initiative through a responsible mind-set. Dixon doesn't beat herself up or get defensive when she sees bad news, or when gets feedback that indicates she's off course. She uses the information to take action. In fact, once her firm got low scores—fifty out of one hundred—on the training and development section of the survey. This piqued her attention since she had tripled the training budget. Because Dixon had a learning mind-set, she used the information like a detective to uncover new information.

Aligning Meaning

It would have been easy for Dixon to ignore the feedback on the survey or take the feedback personally—after all, she had increased the training budget, so why the lousy scores? Instead, she decided to dig a little deeper:

> I arranged a task force made up of the age group [I was targeting] and I said to them, "What would a world of perfect training look like for you?" I just listened. The most interesting thing occurred. Their definition of training and my definition of training are very different. Their definition, for the twenty-three of them across the board, was that they

wanted to pick the training opportunity in their particular discipline, let's say public relations, and they wanted to be sent off for a week to Las Vegas or New York. It's certainly industry training but also packaged in with a heck of a lot of fun.[14]

Dixon's definition of training was to help team members gain knowledge or expertise in areas where they needed to grow, for example, sending them to Dale Carnegie Training to sharpen their presentation skills or setting up a webinar in the conference room to train in social media.

Getting everyone aligned and using the same definitions for training did the trick. "From then on, every single Wednesday I would say, 'Okay, in the next thirty days we have all of these training opportunities. This week we have a training opportunity that includes a webinar,' and so on. I associated training with all of the things that we were currently doing but I called them training,"[15] she said. As leaders, the way we use language can dramatically change perceptions, alignment, and cooperation. As a result, employees are more aware of the real opportunities available to them, and how those opportunities meet their development needs.

Aligned, Aware, and Accountable

This is a simple example of how alignment and awareness work with accountability. If the language, definitions, or measurements we use are not congruent (aligned) we create misunderstanding. When misunderstandings erupt, it's easy to lose self-awareness and get defensive. Dixon said she almost fell to the ground when she saw the scores. A less aware leader might lead by emotion and place blame. The knee-jerk reaction would be to blame Gen X or Y workers or to let resentment fester without clarifying the interpretations.

On the other side of the awareness spectrum, leaders who are too "others-aware" might go ahead and send employees to Vegas for "training" without determining whether that training was the best option for developing their talent. Instead, Dixon became curious. She put together a task force, asked questions, and listened.

Here we see evidence of responsible growth orientation married to accountability—the willingness to look at potentially unpleasant information. We see the awareness of self and others as well as a high spiritual awareness, which makes sure the decisions are aligned with the values and goals of the company. Third, we see alignment through education—Dixon's approach reinforced a common language that identified when training had taken place and reiterated the importance of accountability.

Layers of Leadership and Accountability

Depending on the corporate structure, larger companies experience different challenges with accountability because of the layers of leadership. For example, a manager might not feel the urgency to do a critique of an employee if it's easy to transfer the employee to another department. The more removed the leader is from the responsibility of revenue, the less inclined she is to correct performance issues, especially when she has not been given the knowledge or resources to do so.

Regarding the small business owner, it's a common misconception that owners are highly motivated to be accountable and to learn the leadership skills necessary to run their companies, as Lauren Dixon has. After all, their investment is on the line. However, from my observation, many owners with high financial stakes still struggle with accountability. The real issue is one of *responsibility*, not *accountability*. One cannot be truly accountable until a responsible mind-set has been adopted. When the leader adopts a responsible mind-set and then becomes accountable, she has the power to develop responsible and accountable employees.

The lack of leadership accountability contributes to unnecessary workplace drama. One of the biggest failures of accountability in leadership positions at every level happens when the leader avoids having difficult conversations. The problem is when the leader tries to nip drama in the bud instead of pulling it out by the roots. Here is how to recognize the bud-nipping in the form of observable behaviors:

- Moving the problem employee to another department.
- Promoting the incompetent employee to management.
- Giving the employee an impossible assignment to show who is boss.
- Transferring the problem to another manager.
- Over-compensating or appeasing a difficult employee.
- Letting the star performer get by with poor team behaviors.

Cracking the Code on Accountability

Core elements must be in place for accountability to be effective.

1. Vision, mission, and stated values
2. Knowledge and resources
3. Responsibility
4. Tools
5. Witness
6. Growth mind-set

First, you must have firmly in place your vision, mission, and core values, all necessary elements for clarity and alignment. Second, you must have knowledge and resources to do the job. Third, is taking ownership through responsibility. Fourth, you must have in place effective tools to measure current reality against the intended outcome. The tools might be a sales report, a set of scales, or a measuring tape. Fifth is a witness. The witness is usually someone to report to, a pair of eyes to interpret the data and report the information. The sixth element is the growth mind-set; this is the glue that holds together the other core elements. The growth mind-set, as described by Dweck, contributes to a transparent and open culture, eliminates the judgment that blocks truth telling, and keeps us from the eyes to see.

Executive Summary

➤ There are distinctions between accountability and responsibility.
➤ Responsibility is the bridge between alignment and accountability.
➤ Those who have a growth mind-set believe they can develop themselves.
➤ Those who have a fixed mind-set believe intelligence and growth are carved in stone.

Wisdom Exercises

1. Ask an employee what accountability means to him and listen for emotion.
2. Describe a time when you actually wanted to measure your progress.
3. Describe a time you simply complied with measuring your progress.
4. List the things in your life you are joyfully responsible for.

PART 2

Eyes to See

Leadership is communicating to people their worth and potential so clearly that they come to see it in themselves.
—Stephen R. Covey

The executives at the supermarket chain didn't invite Harold to attend the merchandising convention in Las Vegas, nor did they seek to gain wisdom from his thirty years as the store's meat manager. Upon their return, the executives told Harold to rearrange the turkey display—to move the cutlets to the end of the aisle, away from the ground turkey where they had been displayed for ten years.

The executives expected increased sales and customer convenience. Instead of selling more cutlets, the store lost money on the out-of-date product left at end of the aisle, unnoticed by customers. "Last week we had to throw away four packages of expired food because people couldn't find what they wanted. That has never happened until they made me change the display," Harold told me.

Every single day executives make decisions without considering the individuals affected by those decisions. These errors in judgment are due to an inability to see: the inability to see the value that each person brings to the workplace; the inability to see the damage done by discounting the opinions of people who are in the trenches doing the work every day; and the inability to see the talent and intellectual capital available.

We can only see what we believe to be true or possible. Neuropsychologist Dr. Kevin Fleming, author of *The Half-Truth High,* once told me, "You are getting 200 million bits of information every nanosecond, and you can only process 5 percent. This means 95 percent of the world is actually passing you by."[1]

Enlightened leaders see more for others than others are able to see for themselves. They master the ability to see different perspectives. Enlightened leaders see how the mistakes that others make offer valuable lessons, and they don't repeat those mistakes. Enlightened leaders consider the short-term, mid-range, and long-term views.

Enlightened leaders see course correction as a competitive advantage—the corrections are done so often that the practice becomes preventive and intentional rather than a reaction to drama. Making tiny shifts, whether in their leadership role or their personal life, becomes a way of being for enlightened leaders. It's not a sign of weakness to admit a mistake but a sign of personal power, an invisible competitive advantage born of integrity and character.

When the enlightened leader experiences unwanted or unexpected change—because of the economy, outside circumstances, or a personal tragedy—he sees the change not as an obstacle but as an opportunity for personal and leadership growth.

Enlightened leaders use communication to understand the perspectives of all stakeholders and shareholders: their language is forward moving and responsible. They represent the company well, seeing communication as an extension of their brand. Enlightened leaders see communication as more than just a soft skill: they see it as a relationship building tool, a branding tool, and as a strategy.

CHAPTER 4

Communication

The single biggest problem in communication is the illusion that it has taken place.

—George Bernard Shaw

Kenneth, an emergency management director, had a lot on his plate. He'd just gotten notice that payroll was $20,000 over budget because of overtime. He promptly called a meeting to tell all eighty employees that their work schedules would be changing. Instead of working twenty-four hours on and seventy-two off, they would now be required to work a daily twelve-hour shift.[1]

Kenneth did not consider that his EMS team members might have some suggestions for scheduling, nor did he tell them why he'd made the decision. As a result, the time he saved with his swift decision making ended up costing him in time and productivity. For the next three months, he dealt with negativity, absenteeism, and turnover, and had to spend time monitoring the social media where employees and past employees gathered to broadcast their situation to the world.

Every day, managers make financial decisions without considering all the facts and how the decisions will affect overall operations.

While they may have mastered the spreadsheet and budget, they lack critical thinking and strategic communication skills.

What is interesting is that companies invest millions of dollars in training to boost technical skills, sometimes called hard skills, while often discounting communication skills training as a nice to have but not necessary.

Seeing Communication Differently

At the corporate level, categorizing communication as a soft skill reduces the likelihood that training for that skill makes it in the budget. However, when we awaken to the fact that all areas of business, including sales, change management, negotiations, and relationship building, require communication mastery, the priority changes from small to significant. This shift in perception changes not only the individual's motivation but the likelihood of budgeting for this type of development.

To be fair, it's understandable that companies don't invest in the development of communication skills: many skills-related courses focus on tactical skills only and do not offer the personal development and coaching often needed to make communication skills effective. You simply cannot master communication skills without developing yourself personally and without a high degree of self- and other-awareness. Communication mastery is about perceiving the meta-messages underneath the requests. It's about listening for inflection and specific language, and spotting the nuances that help you to interpret or clarify the real need. This type of development does not occur in a four-hour webinar; it takes commitment, ongoing development, and daily practice. Enlightened leaders see communication as a relationship builder, a personal branding strategy, and a vehicle for personal growth.

Communication As a Relationship Builder

When communication is viewed as a soft skill, we have missed the fact that business is about building relationships and that communication is the vehicle. Every enlightened leader I have ever met, no matter her level within the company, knows how to connect the dots between communication, business success, and relationship building. I have had many opportunities to talk to successful business leaders who shared the belief that business is not about the financials but about relationships. If you want to understand a CEO's values, listen to her language. In chapter 1, I introduced Bob Funk, CEO and chairman of the board of Express Employment Professionals. He shared his philosophy with me:

> First of all, you have to go out and get customers. That's all about relationships. In our case, we've got two customers. We've got the companies that need good people, and then we have employees who need good jobs. It's a double relationship. The franchises that don't understand that will not be successful. They don't grasp the concept that business is about relationships.[2]

A white paper produced by Express Employment Professionals states that one of the top threats facing business today is poor leadership and communication.[3] Companies often think of relationships in terms of client relationships, but they forget that deeper within the organization exist boss–employee relationships.

Bob continued, "I've seen companies that have not had the best products but have been very successful because they've hired the best people, and they took good care of them. Then, I've seen other companies that have had great products and great service ability but just didn't realize that it's a people relationship not a financial relationship."[4]

The best tool for relationship building is good communication. Effective communication techniques can include:

- Being curious about the other person
- Showing genuine interest
- Listening to the other person's business need
- Shifting focus to gain understanding from various stakeholders
- Following through on promises
- Eliminating gossip and blaming language
- Showing respect

Workplace Relationships and Communication

Anyone who has ever been an employee probably knows what it's like to be told, "I didn't ask you to work here. If you don't like it, find another place to work." This type of behavior and language is anything but relationship building and is toxic to the culture. It is imperative to build leaders who know how to influence employees to be their best selves, rather than make the assumptions that supervisors and managers know these things.

When a leader says to an employee, "I'll get back to you," and then fails to follow through on the promise, trust starts to erode. Sometimes the habit is unintentional and indicates a disorganized life. At other times the action is a way to brush someone off rather than face the difficulty of saying "no." These are not just touchy-feely soft-skills mistakes. These are leadership issues that affect productivity every single day. A disgruntled employee or even just an ornery one can put a serious dent in the brand of the company and can cost the company literally hundreds of thousands of dollars with just a few posts on social media.

Restaurants are extremely vulnerable. At a Domino's Pizza

location, an employee posted videos of himself blowing his nose on a sandwich he was fixing. Frontline supervisors have a great responsibility to look out for the best interests of the company, yet they are offered very little leadership development. Therefore, they experience an identity crisis. Because many supervisors have been promoted from within the workplace, they still identify with those they must oversee, their former coworkers on the front lines. They do not yet identify with being a leader even though they have the title. To transform the culture, those in frontline leadership positions must undergo an identity shift. Instead of viewing themselves as supervisors, they must view themselves as leaders. In today's world, this means that frontline supervisors must be committed to leadership development and training.

Leaders at all levels need to connect and communicate with employees. When supervisors, managers, and C-suite leaders talk to frontline employees, employees take notice. The words, behaviors, and emotional intensity of the leader send a message to that employee about the leader and whether the leader can be trusted.

Stephen Covey, author of *The Speed of Trust* and a top thought leader on the impact of trust in the workplace, says, "Without trust everything gets bogged down, slows down; people protect themselves. You hardly even have to finish sentences when there's high trust. The speed of trust is an amazing thing."[5]

Communication habits like eye rolling, the silent treatment, procrastinating, hinting, or avoiding stain your personal and leadership brands. Enlightened leaders trade these negative manipulative techniques for more conscious and strategic communication. When those at the higher levels become curious about their team members, employees, or associates, they express genuine interest, which promotes engagement, as we will explore in chapter 8. One of the very best relationship-building tools, one that goes deeper than listening, is truly seeing others.

Seeing More for Others

Enlightened leaders use what I call Super Vision. It is the practice of honoring the person in your presence, the practice of seeing something in the person that perhaps he has not seen in himself. This ability is not an innate skill but something that absolutely can be learned. Leaders who use Super Vision understand employees as more than a means to an end; they recognize employees' intrinsic value and believe each worker can offer even more value to the company.

There is scientific evidence to support the idea that the way we see ourselves and the way we see others influences our relationships. The best advice I can give here is to work at viewing everyone as equal in value. Whatever her title, pay scale, talent, or intelligence, every human being is equal in value and deserves respect. While it's true you may only want to partner with certain people, you don't have to discount other people's humanity, criticize their choices, or elevate yourself above them.

Before he passed away, I interviewed Dr. David Simon, a neurosurgeon and former director of the Chopra Center in Carlsbad, California. Dr. Simon shared his seven principles of enlightened relationships. The first principle, he said, "Is that my relationships are based upon equality." Dr. Simon's advice was to experiment with the principle in this way: "Next time you are in a restaurant and a waitress is running around because they are understaffed, say to yourself, 'You and I are the same being in disguise.' The waitress will change her demeanor because she is being seen, and as a result she will change how she delivers service to you."[6]

Very often I practice this skill: the art of really seeing others and seeing their successes that others may not notice. For example, I often meet cab drivers in big cities. By showing genuine interest in the driver, I learn that he has come from another country, secured a job, learned a new language, and sends money back to his family to support a sibling who wants to go to college and build a better life.

One of the greatest skills a leader can learn is to really see others and honor them. It is amazing how we miss the success and potential of other people—including our employees, our bosses, and our associates—because we have labeled them and put them in our mental box. The impact a supervisor, manager, or executive can have on an individual's success can be a turning point in his career, but we may never fully understand the magnitude.

Elaine Brink, executive vice president of Express Employment Professionals, shared with me Bob Funk's ability to see more in others than they see in themselves. She said, "Bob has this innate ability to see more than one ever sees in himself. No one gets hired without an interview with Bob, even though he is the CEO and has a heavy calendar. Under his leadership, Express has put more than six million people to work worldwide."[7]

In essence, you cannot *not* communicate. The behaviors, language, and decisions of the leader are as significant as a branding campaign. Leaders are walking commercials for the companies they work for.

Communication As Your Brand

In May 2013, Cheerios, a division of General Mills, produced an ad featuring a biracial family that included a white mother, a black father, and their little girl, Gracie. The ad caused such a fiery spark of racial debate on General Mills' YouTube channel that the company disabled the comment function. When Cheerios produced a second commercial with the same family to air on Super Bowl Sunday the following year, it communicated a deliberate message to the world: we value diversity, family, and health. The company also communicated a meta-message: we will not be bullied.

Major companies put a lot of conscious thought and deliberate action into what, how, and when they communicate. These companies devote millions of dollars in resources and entire teams of human talent to create the right messaging to represent their brands. From the actors who play roles on television commercials to the sound of an announcer's voice to the exact language and music used, as well as the colors selected for the product's packaging, the company is aiming to plant a positive memory and feeling in the minds and hearts of customers. This is called branding.

Every day, leaders send out messages that communicate—to employees, vendors, strategic partners, and clients—who they are and what they stand for. Right or wrong, employees respond to the brands of their leaders just as they respond to the brand when they watch a Cheerios commercial. The point is, the leader is being judged every single day. The language she uses, the decisions she makes, and the actions she takes broadcast to the world the values, likeability, and trustworthiness of the leader.

In today's world, where every disgruntled customer has access to her own broadcast channel through social media, it is imperative for leaders at every level to gain the wisdom needed to deal with mistakes, manage complaints, and understand the meta-messages clients give when they are upset. Office Max learned a hard lesson about listening to underlying messages from customers when it purchased a database that spun out an insensitive mailing, which resulted in unwanted press.

On a cold January day, Mike Seay went to the mailbox and was shocked to see a letter from Office Max addressed to "Mike Seay, daughter killed in car crash, or current business."[8] Seay contacted Office Max and demanded an explanation. He got his explanation in a statement delivered by an Office Max associate, who said that the problem was a marketing mistake that occurred because the company had purchased a list from a third party. The Office Max representative did not interpret the meta-message—that Mike Seay did not want only an explanation, he wanted an apology. The result was unwanted media attention.

From the perspective of the company, the incident could have happened to any business that uses direct mail marketing. But the mistake wasn't the real problem in this case. Rather, the mistake was that once an upset Seay had called, the company representative failed to consider the customer's perspective and his experience of the mailing piece as a painful reminder of his daughter's death. The representative missed an opportunity to show compassion and genuine concern. As a result, he put the brand at risk. The eyes to see—the ability to take a breath and see a different perspective—is a learned skill that can and should be taught at all leadership levels.

Developing enlightened leaders at all levels reduces some of the risk employers face every day because of the volatile combination of employees' access to social media with their possible bad judgment, poor supervision, and inadequate company policy. An employee's fun and games can become an employer's nightmare, as demonstrated by the example I mentioned earlier, in which a Domino's Pizza employee posted videos of himself blowing his nose into a sandwich. Good policies are designed to communicate boundaries, but it takes enlightened leaders with perspective to determine appropriate actions that align the company's values and the company's brand. An enlightened leader uses communication and relationship-building skills to promote collaboration and commitment rather than contention.

From a personal perspective, we communicate every day through social media without realizing that social media is not just for connection; it is a communication tool that brands you. The rant you post today on Facebook can leave a digital footprint for the rest of your life. Have too much to drink at a party? Someone can snap a picture of you in a compromising position, and in two seconds your reputation is at risk. You certainly did not intentionally communicate that you make bad decisions, yet that's what people will think when they see the pictures with funny captions. It's easy to forget that privacy is a thing of the past, and what you post today you could regret tomorrow.

A professor at East Stroudsburg University in Pennsylvania, Dr. Gloria Gadsden, was suspended after updating her Facebook status with posts such as, "Does anyone know where I can find a very discrete [*sic*] hit man? Yes, it's been that kind of day."[9] The university said it was being overcautious because of an earlier shooting incident at the University of Alabama in which three professors were killed by a coworker.

Young leaders and potential leaders who grew up with social media often do not realize the impact of the decisions they make while in their twenties; incidents and comments captured on social media can come back to harm them in their thirties or beyond. Now more than ever, this new freedom calls for a higher level of consciousness and personal responsibility.

The fact is, we are always communicating, whether we are aware of it or not, and our communication affects the way others view us. Enlightened leaders understand that strong communication skills are more than nice-to-have, touchy-feely soft skills; communication is a strategy essential for branding, negotiating, and building business relationships, as well as for continued personal growth.

Communication As a Strategy

Strategy should always support the big vision and the desired result. Yet we often forget to connect the strategy dots between relationships and results. Here are some questions to consider: Is it better to make a quick decision to save time or to consider other points of view before deciding? Is it more productive to talk to an employee about a difficult situation soon after it occurs, or should you wait until the employee joins the union, achieves tenure, or has twenty years' seniority? Do you build more trust by telling someone something he wants to hear, only to have to disappoint him later, or do you build more trust by speaking honestly from the start about your level of interest? As a leader, do you gain more respect by laughing at offensive jokes or do you gain respect by representing yourself as someone who will not tolerate racism, sexism, or disrespect toward any individual?

When it comes to aligning relationship building and desired results, "being right" should not be your desired end result, from a strategic point of view. When you are determined from the outset to prove your point and make the other person wrong, you have already lost. It is not strategic to seem to agree with someone when you don't, pretend things are okay when they aren't, or persuade someone to do something that is against her core values. These tactics are manipulative, and there is a deep gulf between manipulation and strategy.

What makes communication strategic? Strategic communication requires three things:

1. Knowing your intended result
2. Understanding the viewpoints of the other stakeholders
3. Representing yourself in alignment with your brand

If you are not clear about your intended result, your communication will be reactive or you will be dragged off course by other people's agendas. If your communication supports the result but tricks the other person or is not a mutual win, then it's manipulative and not strategic. If, in the end, you sacrifice your values to get to the desired result, you will be out of alignment. Using communication as a strategy means embracing and practicing the three Cs: clarity, curiosity, and communication.

Clarity

The biggest source of drama is lack of clarity about your desires, objectives, or intended result. This is true whether you are a middle-level leader preparing for a difficult conversation with an employee or a top-level executive negotiating a million-dollar business deal. If you don't know what you want, any wind will sway you and you'll waste enormous amounts of time following everyone else's agenda. Here are three questions you can ask yourself to help gain clarity:

1. What result do I desire?
2. Am I completely honest and transparent about my agenda?
3. Do these desires align with my values?

After you become clear about your desires, honest in your agenda, and you are aligned with your values, you must be careful not to make assumptions about the other individuals involved. This may require some investigation, fact finding, relationship building, or listening, depending on the situation. For example, if you are communicating in a sales negotiation, your actions may be different than if you are using communication as a strategy to deal with an employee performance issue. Nonetheless, you must maintain clarity while remembering to shift your perspective to see all points of view.

Kenneth, the EMS director who needed to cut overtime in his department, was very clear about his desired result. But he failed to consider and consult the other people involved before making his final decision. In fact, Kenneth had recently disciplined two crews caught napping while on duty. If he had investigated a little before disciplining the crews, Kenneth would have discovered that crews in certain areas run more medical calls of service than those working in low-call-volume areas. During the course of a shift, employees in high-volume areas must handle out-of-county transports that require advanced life-support monitoring. With a limited amount of downtime for rest, these employees are at a higher risk for being involved accidents or providing inadequate patient care. Taking a quick nap was a conscious decision designed to manage energy. The lack of communication between boss and employee created unnecessary drama.

You must seek to understand all the stakeholders in any situation: your boss, associates, employees, customers, or vendors. Now, it's time to get curious.

Curiosity

Curiosity communicates that you have other people's best interests at heart, in addition to your own. This requires you to be open to learning by doing two things: listening and asking questions. You must let go of your agenda momentarily, which requires that you have the awareness to notice when you tend to manipulate or react.

Curiosity means more than asking a good question. Curiosity means asking a question, then listening while the other person speaks. The one who listens controls the conversation. Remember the statement, "When I talk, I know what I know, but when you talk, I know what I know, and I know what you know." You are aiming to increase your knowledge and understanding. You are looking for some sort of common ground, some sort of connection to provide a starting place from which to build a relationship. You are trying to connect the dots. If you skip this step, you will most likely have a very difficult time or you will fail altogether.

Especially when it comes to negotiations or sales, one of the biggest strategic mistakes is to speak too quickly about your agenda. It's dangerous to start talking about what you want or will do until you understand the other parties involved. You don't have enough information to know how to approach the conversation, nor do you know enough or care enough about what they want to reach common ground. You might think your rambling is harmless, but it can drive others away if they are uncomfortable with negotiations. Or, if you are using communication as a strategy with an employee, you set up defensiveness if you start talking about performance without considering the facts and understanding the employee's position.

There are only three ways to reach common ground. The first is to convince the other party or parties to align completely with your desires. The second way is for you to completely align with theirs. The third way is to negotiate—to decide how much you are willing to adjust and how much the other party is willing to adjust. Before you speak about your desires or intentions, see if there is the potential to come together.

Communication: A Strategic Model

I have developed a Strategic Communication Model that will help you visualize alignment versus misalignment. From your starting point, indicated by the black dot, a straight line leads to your desired end result, A. Regarding alignment, B is closer to A; therefore, B is more closely aligned with A than C, D, and E. As you can see, point C is about 90 degrees away from A. This model is intended to help guide you intuitively by giving you a method to visualize how far apart you are from someone else's intentions, agenda, or goal. The key is to experiment with the model, visualizing where you are versus where she is while listening to her agenda. With practice you will get a sense if there is room for negotiation and how wide the gap. Experiment by thinking about a time in the past when you simply could not work with the other person, even though you saw the potential in the beginning. If you have experienced a huge disappointment you will see by using this model that you either didn't listen, or you tried to press on even when your objectives were not aligned. If what you want is at point A, and the other person is at point E, chances are you are wasting time trying to align.

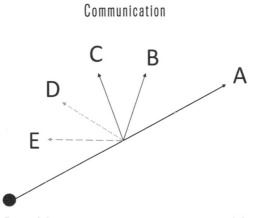

Figure 4-1: Strategic Communication Model

Notice that D and E are broken lines. The broken lines indicate red flag areas with virtually no opportunity for alignment. This is because both D and E are more than 90 degrees away from A. In fact, D is about 120 degrees off and E is about 140 degrees away. When you are seeking alignment, whether your goal is to improve an employee's performance or to negotiate a big sale, you want to know where the other person's intentions and interests are compared with yours. For example, if you are trying to improve an employee's performance but he is resistant, he is 180 degrees off course (heading in the exact opposite direction of your desired result). If he is also unwilling to change his attitude or get the coaching or skills he needs, it is apparent that it will be most productive to cut ties. The same principle applies to negotiating with a potential partner.

Before talking or telling, listen. Get curious. You already know your values, mission, and objective. Now spend time listening and asking good questions to learn the other party's values and goals. When you get good at this, it will almost seem like you are hearing radar blips go off. When the other person is speaking your language, there is resonance: *boop, boop, boop.* Don't get too excited. Keep listening and learning! When the other person's language is more than 90 degrees off course from your goal, it sounds like a flat line: *beeeeeeep*. Before long, your intuition will develop and you will be able to read others' communication for alignment. It gets easier with practice.

If any stakeholder is more than 90 degrees out of alignment, it may simply be due to a lack of understanding. Enlightened leaders have the ability to see their stakeholders as partners, not as adversaries, even when there is initial pushback. Understanding can shift an individual from 150 degrees away to just a few degrees off course, or even to full alignment. If, however, you are not able to get an appropriate degree of alignment after communicating strategically, it's going to take a lot of compromising on one side, the other, or both. The best opportunities are when the values and objectives are close rather than far apart.

Agreement and Alignment

It's unlikely you can persuade someone to your way of thinking if her core values are not at all aligned with yours or if your interests are in direct conflict with hers. If, however, you can find agreement within an acceptable range, then it's simply about one or both of you moving toward agreement. Once you know what you want, it's easier to change course three degrees, twenty degrees, or even sixty degrees by conscious choice. If you are unclear about what you want, you can get dragged along by someone else's agenda. The method of "I'll know it when I see it" will likely waste a lot of time, and will ultimately result in someone feeling resentful—probably you.

Representing Your Brand

Now that you understand the strategic nature of communication, it's time to choose a powerful, positive, and forward-moving communication style that truly represents brand *You*. If you value integrity, you can't behave like a slick salesperson just to close the deal. Your inner guidance and spiritual awareness won't allow you to take advantage of one who is less savvy or less aware. Your communication is about you and the other party finding agreement, which requires that you don't allow yourself to get off course on a hidden agenda or manipulate the other person to act against his best interests. Nothing happens if both parties have their heels dug in.

Willingness is the fulcrum point of change. If the other party is unwilling to negotiate at all, you must be willing to do all the compromising. Your ability to communicate can be the competitive advantage, whether you want to keep employees aligned with the mission, negotiate a sale, or build a business. The good news is that any area in which you think you might have failed points to an opportunity for you to become a more competent and strategic communicator. Enlightened leaders use communication as a tool for personal growth.

Communication As a Tool for Personal Growth

No matter what the company budget, every leader has the power to improve his communication skills if he is willing to work on the new skill or mind-set until the habit crystallizes. Start with these three essential leadership communication skills:

- Trading reactive language for responsible language
- Speaking into the future instead of into the past
- Asking for what you want

Enlightened leaders use **responsible language** rather than reactive or manipulative language. The benefits to the leader go beyond increased leadership competence. You also learn to listen for red flags that indicate an employee is not willing to be responsible and, therefore, not willing to be accountable. You'll become aware of reactive body language in yourself or in others as well—mannerisms that indicate a button has been pushed, like eye rolling, a heavy sigh, folded arms, or some other expression of frustration. When these behaviors are unconscious, they are simply reactive—an automatic response done without conscious thought. Reactive communication is about relief in the short term and takes less energy than conscious thought.

When we make promises we know we aren't going to keep, we are using manipulation. Our intention is to make someone feel good in the moment. When we make a promise but are unaware of our habit of breaking promises, we are behaving in a reactive and unconscious way. Here is a short list of such reactive behaviors:

- Eye rolling
- The silent treatment
- Forgetting
- Passive-aggressive behavior
- Hinting
- Avoiding
- Pretending
- Game playing

Self-awareness, which I talked about in chapter 1, is a prerequisite for using responsible and nonreactive language. To become more self-aware, stop and observe your inner dialogue. Your inner dialogue automatically transfers outwardly and manifests in the words you speak. Phrases like "It's not fair" and "I had no choice" indicate that a victim mind-set has taken form and crystallized into language. Enlightened leaders take responsibility for their thoughts, feelings, and language. It is not easy, and the process is more a journey of course correction than perfection, but the bottom line is this: enlightened leaders cannot afford to use irresponsible, reactive, or manipulative language.

Speaking into the Future

A close cousin to reactive language is what I call backward-moving language. When we consistently talk about what should not have been done or what has always been done or how someone messed up years ago, we speak about the past instead of the future. In marriage, these communication habits are called nagging. In companies, they are called feedback.

Most of us avoid asking for feedback. When someone asks you, "May I give you some feedback?" you may experience a queasy stomach for a moment before catching your breath and saying, "Sure!" But the truth is, most people respond favorably to suggestions for minor tweaks or course corrections they can use for better performance in the future. If you are on the receiving end of negative feedback, avoid defensiveness. That skill will help keep communication flowing and give you the opportunity to suggest changes or fine-tuning for superior performance in the future.

I love executive coach Marshall Goldsmith's term "feed forward."[10] When we talk about the future, we inspire people to a new vision. When we continue to focus and talk about the past, we contribute to toxic energy; we would do better to talk about the vision, the future, and fresh possibilities. Most people are more than happy to have dialogues about improvements, shifts, and course corrections. Similarly, they naturally want to avoid getting beaten down by ruminations over past mistakes that should have been long buried.

Asking for What You Want

Most people simply can't bring themselves to ask for what they want. Because it's easier to notice poor communication habits in others, here is a quick exercise: the next time you hear an employee complaining, listen and acknowledge his frustration; then, once the employee feels heard, stop and ask, "What is it that you want?" Instead of an answer, I predict that you will hear about what's not working, why something isn't fair, or why things will never change. You also will hear a long laundry lists of "what I don't want." In fact, most people will say, "I don't want to argue" rather than "I want to get along."

Talking about what you don't want is draining, while talking about what you do want is energizing. Talking about what you don't want can be confusing, while talking about what you want is clear and direct. Whatever you focus on expands, so focusing on what you do not want only creates more awareness of it, which is a bottomless pit. It is rare to hear anyone answer the question "What do you want?" with a clear, positive statement. Until you are clear about what you want, you won't get it. Until you are clear about what you want from your employees, associates, or colleagues, and can communicate it, they can't measure up. Clarity is king when it comes to communication.

In all areas of life, you need to communicate. You need to be able to explain, clarify, gain cooperation, seal the deal, heal misunderstandings, and build new relationships. You need to be able to relate to all kinds of people; those of higher status, lower status, or equal status, as perceived by society and yourself.

You need to be competent in using many tools of communication, including e-mail, texting, and telephones. You have to constantly work with people who communicate poorly; are less aware of their emotions; and are very short sighted, impatient, self-serving, or less than articulate. Doesn't it make sense strategically for you as a leader to develop your communication skills to bridge the gaps, making yourself as aware, capable, articulate, and strategic as you can be?

Executive Summary

➤ We are always communicating, whether we know it or not.
➤ Clarity and curiosity are prerequisites for strategic communication.
➤ The ability to see others clearly can be learned and practiced.
➤ Knowing what you want is the first step in strategic communication.

Wisdom Exercises

1. Practice asking people what they want, and write down their replies and your observations.
2. Before your next meeting or activity, write down what you want to happen.
3. Describe a time when you reacted instead of communicating strategically.

CHAPTER 5

Change

Change always involves a dark night when everything falls apart. Yet if this period of dissolution is used to create new meaning, then chaos ends and new order emerges.

—Margaret Wheatley

Employees at International Harvester Renew Center knew something was wrong. They kept asking plant manager Jack Stack what to expect: "Is this a good time to buy a house?" "Should I get married?" "Should my spouse and I go ahead and have a child?" Stack didn't want to answer those questions because he alone knew he had come to Missouri to close down the Springfield plant.

Stack knew his mission would affect the lives of the employees who showed up every day to clean, repair, and replace used transportation products. The company rebuilt parts to their original quality for potential clients in the agriculture, defense, and automotive industries. Even with all the efforts of those at the Springfield plant, International Harvester was in deep financial trouble. With a debt of more than $6 billion owed to two hundred banks, the parent company was hemorrhaging cash and the Springfield plant was not part of the core business, so Stack and the employees knew change was on the horizon.

There is a common myth that people resist change. The reality is that most people are willing to embrace change when they are in charge of the change or when they believe the change offers expansion and growth. People get married, have children, buy new homes, move across the country, and start businesses. They pay off debt, lose weight, give up addictions, and run marathons, even though the changes are difficult mentally, physically, or spiritually. The kind of change people resist is change that is imposed upon them against their wishes, change that is unwanted, unexpected, or forced.

The workers at the Springfield plant were going through an unwanted change completely beyond their control. They knew that eventually they would all lose their jobs. It seemed as though there were no choices.

Denise Bredfeldt, one of the few women working in the plant, had been hired to build hydraulic pumps, valves, and cylinders. She recalled the early days at Harvester: "The first couple of years were nothing but show and tell to get dealers to understand the remanufacturing process, and why it was a good deal for them to purchase. It was kind of a joke, because we took apart one cylinder for one group and put it back together for the next group. There wasn't a whole bunch of production that went on for about two to three years."[1]

Even though the plant workers were putting in a lot of effort, they lacked direction and leadership as well as some manufacturing finesse. Bredfeldt described those early meetings when Stack would meet with all the employees to update them on the status: "Jack said that he was sent to find out if we could be profitable, and actually make money. Depending on what he found out, that there would be action taken one way or another. It was, maybe six months, eight months later when he would get the word from Chicago to shut it down. By then, he had taken heart and figured out that we could really do good things if we just had the right help, leadership, and resources."[2]

Dark Night of the Soul

Unwanted change offers a unique opportunity born out of a dark night of the soul. When life looks bleak and you feel backed up against a wall with no choices, the darkest night of desperation always precedes the dawn of transformation. For the Harvester employees, the dark night came with the realization that the plant would likely shut down. For Stack, the dark night came through guilt. After many months of getting to know the hardworking people in the plant, he simply could not make peace with his mission to shut it down. Instead of seeing dispensable plant workers and a factory full of old machine parts, he saw an entrepreneurial spirit and a superior work product. He felt compelled to try *something*, but he could think of no other choice but to fulfill his mandate to close the plant.

Then, amidst the unrest and chaos, something changed. Stack had a moment of enlightenment, and he said, "Why don't we try to buy the company?"[3] He had the *eyes to see* a new possibility, one that had not yet been considered. Galvanized by hope, he embarked upon an odyssey to build capital with the intention of purchasing the plant from International Harvester.

A flash of enlightenment often follows a dark night of the soul and leads to transformation. One struggles with an experience for which there seems to be no solution, then one day a big *aha!* strikes. A light switches on. In the clarity of the light, it's easy to see how all the parts fit together. The meaning of the struggle emerges, the dots are connected. There are lessons to learn, skills to gain, wisdom to share. Enlightened leaders see choice and opportunity for growth, even when they are backed up against the wall. As a result, enlightened leaders transform uncertainty and drama into a noble purpose. The first glimmer occurs when the enlightened leader recognizes choice even when others see no alternatives.

After building a business plan, securing $100,000 in financing, and approaching more than fifty banks, Stack finally found a bank that would loan the money to purchase the plant, which was renamed Springfield Remanufacturing Company, or SRC for short.

Stack started teaching the employees financial literacy. He opened the books and taught them how to read financial statements, how to understand profit and loss, how to know when they were making or losing money, and how to think like entrepreneurs. That entire experience led him to write the book *The Great Game of Business*, the largest and most well-known resource for open-book management training and education.

Other company leaders from across the country wanted to learn how Stack had turned the company around. SRC started offering tours, and eventually The Great Game educational arm of the SRC was born. Today, more than six thousand businesses across the world have experienced the coaching, mentoring, and training services offered by The Great Game of Business.

When we hear the story about Stack, SRC, and the Great Game of Business, we applaud the success and feel inspired momentarily. It's so easy to overlook the trials, the doubt, the stress, and the pressures that Stack and the employees faced for many months in the midst of uncertainty and unwanted change. Wanted or unwanted, expected or unexpected, change offers rich opportunities for leadership growth. That's why I have developed a model for leaders to use that will help them understand where they are and guide their choices as they navigate through the rough waters of change.

Quadrants of Leadership Growth

Using a double axis, where the constant is change, and the two variables are the level of desire and the level of certainty—these are referred to as change that is expected or unexpected on the X axis, and change that is wanted or unwanted on the Y axis.

Change

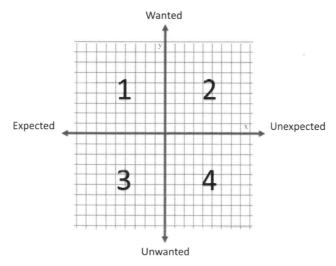

Wanted

1 2

Expected | Unexpected

3 4

Unwanted

Figure 5-1: Four Quadrants of Leadership Growth

Quadrant 1: Expected and wanted change
Quadrant 2: Unexpected but wanted change
Quadrant 3: Expected but unwanted change
Quadrant 4: Unwanted and unexpected change

Looking at each quadrant objectively, we can see that the potential for leadership growth as well as the potential pitfalls differ in each quadrant. Leaders can use this tool to understand how change can be viewed from multiple perspectives: that of their employees, of their associates, and their own. This will help them effectively lead change.

Quadrant 1: Expected and Wanted Change

Life seems wonderful when change is both expected and wanted, as in Quadrant 1. This can happen, for example, when you are starting a business, working for and getting a job promotion, or making life decisions like moving, getting married, or having children.

It is important to note that company leaders may experience a particular change as expected and wanted; that same change may, however, be experienced by employees as unexpected and unwanted. The quadrants model offers a way to see the change from the other stakeholders' perspective and then communicate strategically to manage the change.

In addition to launching an effective communication plan, a significant leadership growth opportunity in Quadrant 1 is to always consider the different perspectives. The third opportunity is to understand that favorable change in one area often leads to unwanted or unexpected change in some other area.

It's easy to become overly confident, fail to plan, or get overwhelmed by all the choices available when the changes are exciting and open up new opportunities. When things are always going your way, it's easy to forget that they can change quickly without your consent or desire. When in this quadrant, the enlightened leader considers other perspectives. What could go wrong? What actions could we take while times are good to take preventive measures and create a contingency plan for when unwanted changes occur.?

Quadrant 2: Unexpected but Wanted Change

You land in Quadrant 2 when you get a surprise you are happy to accept. Unexpected but welcome change can come from within the organization or from the outside environment. Inside the organization, you might get a nice promotion you didn't expect. From outside, perhaps a new law was passed that works in your favor. Once again, as a leader you must consider how your excitement about the change translates to other stakeholders. When good news comes at the expense of a counterpart, vendor, customer, or associate, leaders must be mindful that this change may put the coworkers, associates, or counterparts in Quadrant 3 or 4, which are less auspicious and comfortable.

As in all quadrants, the opportunity for leadership growth requires you to stay alert to how this unexpected change affects other stakeholders, as well as how this unexpected change affects the environment or culture. Quadrant 2 is often the quadrant of hope, where the leader gets a flash of insight.

When Stack of SRC asked, "What if we try to buy this place?," this new thought contributed to a change that would be unexpected but wanted, not only from his perspective but presumably from the employees' perspective as well.

Quadrant 3: Expected but Unwanted Change

Quadrant 3 is the waiting-for-bad-news quadrant. Employees at Harvester knew their plant was slated for closure eventually. The change was unwanted but expected. It is important not to place judgment on the term "unexpected" or the term "unwanted." Just because a change is expected or forewarned does not always make the change tolerable; and just because the change is unwanted does not mean the change is always dramatic or life changing.

As is true in all other quadrants, change that happens in Quadrant 3 can be life altering, or the change can be irrelevant in the scheme of life. In other words, the change can be as dramatic as knowing the plant is going to close or as mundane as knowing you will eventually get wrinkles. In both instances, change is coming, and you know it, even though you don't want the change to occur. I call this quadrant the bad weather quadrant. We complain about the rain even though we knew the forecast and can do nothing about it.

The leadership growth opportunity, for all quadrants but especially Quadrant 3, is to accurately assess the severity and importance of the change. Then, no matter what the level of importance, leaders must face reality, stop wasting energy complaining, and seek to discover new options or develop a different plan. The opportunity for growth is in consciously stopping the habit of resisting change that must be accepted. After acceptance comes the opportunity for the insight.

Quadrant 4: Unexpected and Unwanted Change

Quadrant 4 ranges from disappointment to tragedy. Something catches you off guard and disappoints you. You were blindsided, perhaps overlooked for a promotion you feel you deserved. Or the unexpected and unwanted change may be due to sudden economic shifts, the weather, or some other unforeseen circumstance. You didn't expect the plant to close. Someone died. A tornado came into town and demolished the city. You lost your job without warning. You might be thinking that Quadrant 4 changes come only from outside the environment, but that would be erroneous thinking. A tornado, which is an outside influence, cannot be helped, but closing a plant without warning can be—it just takes the right communication plan to move this out of the "unexpected" category.

Employees who have worked in start-ups with entrepreneurial leaders have told me in informal interviews how their leaders often throw employees into Quadrant 4 through unconscious decision making. Some entrepreneurial leaders promise things that are impossible to deliver, place unreasonable demands on their employees, expect outrageous work hours, and change direction without notice.

Of course, these entrepreneurial start-up leaders do not experience the fourth quadrant because they are the ones who have the choice, the decision-making power, and a bigger stake in the outcome. The opportunities for leadership growth in Quadrant 4 include becoming more deliberate, communicating more often, and managing change more effectively.

From an outside-the-environment perspective, the tornado, fire, or unexpected death offer leadership opportunities: to reexamine and realign values. In this quadrant, it is easy to lose hope and spiral into despair. Quadrant 4 is often the dark-night-of-the-soul quadrant.

Opportunities for personal growth in every quadrant occur through self-analysis, and the opportunity for leadership growth occurs when leaders use the quadrants as a reminder to view change through the eyes of employees. The greatest opportunity for leadership growth occurs when either the level of certainty or the level of choice is threatened. Let's look at certainty first to see how leaders can either dial up or dial down the certainty factor.

Certainty Versus Uncertainty

Quadrants 2 and 4 both deal with uncertainty. A little uncertainty creates excitement, while too much leads to anxiety. Leaders need to understand that everyone has different levels of tolerance regarding uncertainty. With any change comes varying degrees of uncertainty that make the experience of change challenging, exciting, uncomfortable, or almost unbearable.

Most of us can tolerate only so much uncertainty, even if we want change. That is why lottery winners often experience tremendous stress after winning the lottery. They gladly said, "Yes" to the change but didn't know how to live within those changes. Their Quadrant 2 experience shoves them into Quadrant 4: the unexpected and unwanted tax bill, people calling for donations, family squabbles, and the life lessons that come with managing large sums of money.

A business example would be promoting an employee to a management or supervisory position without giving him leadership training. The employee is delighted to get the opportunity. The promotion was an unexpected but wanted change. However, without training, the new leader often spirals down into Quadrant 4 and feels trapped because he has not had the necessary development, mentoring, or experience. Too much of the unexpected contributes to drama and anxiety.

Supervisors and managers who have been in their position for several years are often too afraid to ask for help. They don't want their boss to perceive them as weak. They continue to hide their problem and experience a loss of control.

In Control

The need to feel in control explains why so many people watch the weather forecast, pay for caller ID, and read their daily horoscope. These little signals give a measure of relief in this world of rapid change and uncertainty, so we know whether it's going to rain, who is on the other end of the line, or if the stars are aligned enough to apply for the loan. The brain loves to look for patterns and does so to feel more certain. The brain always wants closure. It's more comfortable to make up a story that closes the loop than it is to say, "I don't know" or "I'm not sure." Intolerance of uncertainty is related to anxiety, panic disorders, and depression. Leaders who are uncertain of how to lead produce uncertainty in their employees.

Most of us don't even like movies if there is uncertainty in the ending. In the continually running movie of our mind, we manage our uncertainty by making up the ending instead of sitting with the unknown. For example, when you schedule a call and the other person isn't available and doesn't call back or reply to your messages, it's easier to judge the person as irresponsible or to assume you must have offended her rather than to admit that you don't have the missing puzzle piece.

"Not knowing" is a problem for the brain. However, the fact is, you may never know why the proposal was not accepted, why the call was not returned, or why you didn't win the award, even if you seek the answers. Enlightened leaders know how to manage the "monkey mind," which chatters constantly in pursuit of understanding. The secret is to stay close to the facts in the midst of uncertainty and remain clear of assumptions and storytelling. Leaders can then use the four quadrants of change model to help employees think critically in the midst of uncertainty instead of reacting.

At some point, every leader, business owner, and entrepreneur experiences change in ways that test her strength and challenge her leadership. It is precisely these experiences that provide an opportunity for the leader to produce new vision, new purpose, and, ultimately, enlightened leadership.

Dialing Up Certainty

There are literally hundreds of ways to dial up the certainty factor for your employees. A clear mission, vision, and values dial up certainty and make decisions easier. A metaphorical North Star provides direction and a plan provides a map. Even though the plan will most certainly change, regular communication and updates help everyone know what to expect. Simply having a short briefing every morning, or at least once every week, can keep everyone on an even keel. This simple practice takes away the ambiguity, so that employees and leaders alike stay focused instead of distracted.

In *Stop Workplace Drama* I introduced a concept called **shortening the gap**,[4] when the project at hand is long and demanding, leaders can create smaller goals that align with the larger goal. Knowing that the plan is likely to shift or even get dropped altogether, a leader can present the entire goal but offer pilot programs for a period of time, then reassess the goals toward the end of the pilot period. This type of change management offers employees a sense of accomplishment so they stay engaged and motivated instead of disheartened by constant volatility that is unplanned, unexpected, and unwanted.

Job descriptions, standard operating procedures, and policies, when used correctly, offer stability and structure in an unstable world and help dial up certainty. Disregarding policies, ignoring job descriptions, and violating standard operating procedures all dial down the certainty. Although there are times when it's necessary to dial down a certainty factor to prepare employees for a coming change, deviating from a healthy structure of policies and standards is not a good way to do it.

When leaders need to create some excitement, they can do so through learning experiences, mentoring, job shadowing, or putting an employee on a new low-risk assignment to develop new skills. Leaders have a great deal of influence in dialing up or dialing down the certainty factor, and enlightened leaders know how to use certainty and uncertainty to their advantage. However, it is in Quadrants 3 and 4 where leaders learn the most about managing unwanted change.

Unwanted Change and Resistance

Expected or not, unwanted change provokes resistance. Resistance always impedes progress; therefore, it is imperative for leaders to understand how to identify resistance and deal with it.

The easiest way to think of resistance is with the acronym SAND: stuck, attached, negative, and distracted. Take any situation where there has been unwanted change, whether it was expected or unexpected, and you will see those who are stuck in the past, stuck about what to do, or stuck thinking about what should have happened that didn't. What often causes "stuckness" is an attachment to the way things should be but aren't. When plans fail, as they often do, leaders make things worse by refusing to alter the plan or to consider contingencies. The root of attachment is the need to be right at all costs, a dangerous trait that quashes innovation and prohibits teamwork.

Once attachment takes root and people get stuck, negativity follows. This is where the perception of what I call **choice poverty** takes root. When people are resistant, they often display signs of a victim mentality—they feel very little hope and do not recognize any viable choices. Choice poverty is what causes people to lose their motivation to align with the corporate mission and goals. The manifestations of choice poverty include negativity, complaining, absenteeism, and, eventually turnover.

Leaders who are uncomfortable with the facts and those who are not equipped to handle employee resistance often resort to distraction. Distraction is the art of avoiding what is important by working on whatever catches your interest at the moment. It's the tendency to get excited about something totally unrelated to the most important matter at hand.

Distractions ease the pain of resistance, but only for the moment. Some of the ways resistance materializes include:

- Negativity
- Complaining
- Lost hope
- Insubordination
- Power struggles
- Backstabbing
- Gossip

We are living in an interesting and paradoxical time when it comes to choices. Most of us are drowning in a sea of choices in almost every area of life, from what to watch on television to what restaurant to choose to what tool to use to manage our workload. People constantly complain of feeling overwhelmed, which is the experience of drowning in a sea of choice. Even though we have more tools to help us increase productivity than ever before, with every choice there is a new demand for more, better, faster, which ultimately leads back to the experience of choice poverty. You can hear the choice-poverty in the language when people talk about how busy they are, thus not recognizing how to choose among equally important priorities. No choice but to stay late. No choice but to work longer hours. No choice but to miss out on the kids' ballgame. The overwhelm of too many choices always leads back to choice-poverty.

In the workplace, many people experience choice poverty every day. Sometimes the choice poverty arises when employees are given an overwhelming amount of work without adequate resources to get the job done. No choice but to struggle. No choice but to feel exhausted. No choice to ask for help. No choice but to believe there are no other choices. At other times, the choice poverty is due to management decisions made without true consideration of the employees the decision affects.

No matter the reason for the choice poverty experience, when people perceive that they are being forced to accept something outside their control or when they are not given the resources to meet the demand, they resist. When people feel that they have no choices, drama erupts. I'm not talking only about threatening situations such as an impending layoff, a downturn in the economy, or a merger that results in a lost title and position. I'm also talking about small situations where people lose their cool because they cannot see their choices.

I worked in a factory on the front lines for over twenty years, at Kraft Foods. I did everything from packing cheese on the production lines, to tearing down equipment for sanitation on third shift Friday nights, to driving a forklift and moving product. Working on the production lines I got to see plenty of drama and choice-poverty. When I worked in the pasta department the work was often tedious and required a chair to do the work comfortably, all it took was someone stealing a coworker's chair to cause a full-blown drama over which person had seniority and what was fair;

the problem then had to be brought before the supervisor, interrupting his work flow. The employee who stole the chair saw no other choice but to take someone else's chair, and the one whose chair was stolen could see no other choice but to tattle. It's not that choices were unavailable. Choices are always available if we have the eyes to see them, however much of the time the cultures in which we work prevent us from recognizing choice. Responsibility includes the recognition of choice. Until people see choice, they simply react to the drama that's capturing their attention, and they look for someone else to fix the problem, which is why the "victim" tattled to the supervisor.

If you think the supervisor had an enlightened response, think again. He told the complainers that if they didn't like it they could "Find another place to work," right after he explained why there was no budget for new chairs. The conversation ended with sage advice about the two choices always available: "Like it or lump it." Lots of time and energy are wasted when no one, including the leadership, sees any viable alternatives. Developing leaders who model choice abundance rather than choice poverty can transform an entire department.

At every level there are always choices. From a front-line perspective a real sign of leadership would be to recognize the choices available. There is the choice of negotiating with others to rotate to one position without a chair in order to be fairer to all. There is a choice to call other departments that may be shut down for the week and borrow a chair.

On the other hand, from a supervisory position, No-Drama Leadership is sometimes simply a matter of justifying the purchase of a couple of new chairs, or facilitating a conversation between the team to figure out a way to change the rotation system to provide a bit of relief. Unfortunately, in my factory experience, the solution was almost always to make the person with less seniority suffer the most pain. This type of problem-solving is short-sighted and always causes unrest among the team members. The point is, no matter what the magnitude of the situation, resistance is due to the inability to see the choice, or to know who the choice actually belongs to. Where you're stuck doesn't matter: a decision about how often to rotate, whether to invest ninety-five bucks for a new chair, or how to save a dying company.

With a choice-abundance mentality, you see idea sharing, sacrifice, and initiative. By contrast, you will never see positive initiative where you see choice poverty. Instead, you will see negative initiative in the form of complaints, excuses, and regrets—all forms of resistance. Resistance slows down progress, wastes time, and increases stress.

Developing leaders who have the ability to see choice even in dire circumstances, and to communicate it to employees, can potentially prevent thousands of dollars' worth of lost productivity due to drama born out of choice poverty. When leaders are able to see from multiple perspectives how unwanted change contributes to resistance, they can intentionally dial up the choice factor.

Dialing Up Choice

Dialing up choice depends on sufficient levels of self-awareness and other-awareness, and on good communication skills. As I said earlier, the leader has to first recognize the signs of resistance and the language that indicates choice poverty. The language of choice poverty is alive and well in most workplaces:

- "That's not possible."
- "It's not my job."
- "I'm just doing my job."
- "I didn't ask you to think."
- "I was backed up against the wall."

- "But you don't understand my situation."
- "I'm too busy."
- "I'm overwhelmed."

Finally, there's the dead giveaway: "I had no choice." There can be no ownership or accountability unless and until you first recognize choice. Most leaders are underdeveloped in listening for resistant the language of choice poverty, and do not know how to inspire those who are in a negative or resistant state. In fact, even high-level executives often use powerless language without realizing it.

Leaders have a great capacity to shift the mind-sets and the language of the workplace by modeling responsible language and asking forward-moving questions. Leaders fall into a trap when they dial down choice by giving advice, telling people what to do, and continuing to focus on the past instead of painting a vision of the future.

Giving Unwanted Advice

Advice giving forces change rather than inviting employees to make the choice for change. Giving unwanted advice often provokes resistance, while coaching promotes awareness and open dialogue. By using coaching techniques rather than directing employees in what to do, you help your employees focus their attention toward the choice rather than toward the problem, thereby encouraging strategic thinking. You are, in effect, helping employees change the way their brains work.

In his book *Your Brain at Work*, David Rock says, "Sensing someone is trying to change you often creates an automatic threat response." He goes on to say, "If being changed by others is usually a threat, this leads to the idea that when real change occurs, it is probably because an individual has chosen to change his own brain."[5] The brain likes to have a choice—more enlightened leaders avoid advice giving and instead offer coaching.

Telling Versus Asking

Another way leaders dial down the choice spectrum is by telling versus asking. Telling someone what his choices are only makes him experience another level of disempowerment and learned helplessness. You hear it all the time from unenlightened leaders, "Well, you have three choices: you can like it, accept it, or find another job." Telling others what their choices are takes them out of responsibility because there is no real ownership.

Edgar Schein, professor emeritus at MIT Sloan School of Management, said in his book *Humble Inquiry*, "I remember being shocked at an answer I received in the classroom. I asked my middle-level executive class at Sloan, what does it mean to you when you get to be promoted to be a manager? You know what most people said? It means I can now tell others what to do."[6] A more enlightened approach is to ask more questions and do less telling. Enlightened leaders see their employees as people who have value instead of robots who are there to take orders.

Schein authored his book to help new leaders understand the value of building relationships in the service of meeting the organizational goals. When I talked with Schein about his book, he said:

The problem I want to solve is how I can get a future boss who is partly dependent on his subordinates because of the complexity of the work, to see his employee as a resource, as a total person, as someone who should be encouraged to speak up rather than beaten down. The way I can think of the boss doing that is inventing ways to interact with his employees that are more egalitarian and that will open up the possibility of some kind of work relationship.[7]

Leaders who build relationships also bolster responsibility. It's difficult for employees to take ownership when they are simply waiting for orders from the boss. Trying to make employees accountable before they take any ownership is a recipe for deception. In contrast, helping employees find choice creates forward movement and focuses attention.

Rather than telling employees what their choices are, it's better to ask, "What are your choices?" Leaders can dial up the choice spectrum by modeling choice abundance and by helping employees take responsibility, encouraging them to acknowledge their choices even in times of struggle or uncertainty. When leaders ask rather than tell, they promote ownership among employees while dialing up the choice factor.

Focusing on the Past

A common mistake leaders make is continuing to focus on the past rather than communicating a vision of the future. The past is what it is. There is no choice in the matter. To continue to give feedback to the employee about what did not happen only contributes to choice poverty.

Even worse than giving feedback to the employee about the past is the habit of talking to others about past problems. Most of the time, there's never been an honest conversation between the leader and employee—and if there has been, there's been no follow-through and no consequence for the poor performance. Leaders I've coached on this matter have a difficult time letting go of their beliefs and past experiences about their problem employees. When I encourage them to have an honest conversation, I hear all manner of irresponsible and resistant language, including, "I already know what she will say," "You just don't understand," and "Let me tell you another story that will convince you I'm right." This is where truth telling comes in handy. You are either willing to help the employee improve or you aren't. If you aren't, you need to find a way to let him go instead of complaining about his poor performance and continuing to dwell on the past.

The tool for transformation is a switch from negative, backward-moving language to positive, forward-moving language. Instead of saying, "I don't want you to make the client angry and lose the account like you did three years ago," the leader would instead say, "My vision is for you to wow the client and secure the account once and for all." The wise leader models responsible language and talks about choices versus obstacles and about the future rather than the past. The language of responsibility always points to choice and to the future.

Schein and I have a common goal: to change the culture surrounding bosses' view of their jobs. "That's what I've tried to do in *Humble Inquiry*," Schein told me, "and it's not going very far. Most of my friends ask, 'How do I get my boss to read it?' "[8]

Schein explained that the best thing I could do is to share my factory experience because it gave me a deep understanding of what it's like to be at the bottom of an organization. "Very few managers have even a clue as to what that's like, and therefore don't have any empathy or humility or any way of thinking about it. If you have an insight into hierarchy from having been there, that's an enormous asset in your own understanding skills," he said.

Jack Stack, plant manager of SRC, and I also have something in common: a background in manufacturing. Even though he was a plant manager in the world of remanufacturing parts for machinery and I was a blue-collar worker on the front lines of a food manufacturer, we can learn from each other. We can see our fellow workers, bosses, colleagues, and associates as valuable resources rather than labeling them by their occupation, age, gender, or title.

At every level of the hierarchy, drama issues tend to be the same at the core: choice poverty versus choice abundance and certainty versus uncertainty during times of change or during times of course correction.

Executive Summary

➢ The dark night of the soul comes before transformation.
➢ Flashes of insight come after the dark night of the soul.
➢ Change always offers opportunity for leadership growth.
➢ Choice poverty can be identified by listening to language.
➢ Dialing up the choice factor promotes responsibility.

Wisdom Exercises

1. Recall a recent work change you have experienced.
2. Identify a quadrant of change as you experienced it.
3. Determine how others might have experienced the same change.
4. Describe how the change affected your leadership ability.

CHAPTER 6

Course Correction

If you think of this world as a place intended simply for our happiness, you find it quite intolerable: think of it as a place of training and correction and it's not so bad.

—C.S. Lewis

On January 10, 2014, Target announced that hackers had stolen financial information for up to seventy million customers.[1] Later, it came to light that, as early as November 2013, a security worker in India had noticed the security breach and notified the Minneapolis operations center. That alert was overlooked. How much trouble could have been avoided if a course correction had taken place the moment the problem was noticed?

One of the most important skills for the enlightened leader is to know when to course-correct. A growth mind-set and a commitment to ongoing leadership development contribute to a culture in which the ability to course-correct swiftly is seen as a competitive advantage, thus increasing productivity and protecting the company from significant risk.

Barriers to Course Correction

One of the greatest challenges for top leaders is creating a culture in which course correction is expected and welcomed as a tool for maintaining alignment. This requires the wisdom to notice the signs, the courage to take actions that effect course correction, and the persistence to overcome the barriers to course correction. Accountability becomes course correction's ally when the leader sees course correction as a competitive advantage rather than something to avoid. Three major barriers to course correction are inconvenience, attachment to the plan, and emotional resistance.

Inconvenience

Look at any case in history, large or small, and you will find that simple inconvenience is a common reason needed corrections did not take place. Sometimes the timing is inconvenient, while at other times the issue is lack of money to fix the problem, a need to increase profits, or a desire to keep someone happy, be it a boss, a customer, or the public. For Target, the "invitation" to course-correct came at the most inopportune time for a retailer—during the holiday season. Warning signs indicating course correction may be necessary often emerge at the worst possible time; therefore, people tend to avoid or deny the need for change while justifying a postponement. The invitation to course-correct always tests your alignment, awareness, and commitment to accountability.

The 1986 explosion of the NASA space shuttle *Challenger* offers a classic example of a team that ignored a warning because of pressure to avoid disappointing the public and an overcommitment to the goal. A course correction in that instance would have required another delay, would have disappointed the public, and possibly would have drawn criticism of the team for failing to complete the mission as planned.

To bring the issue down to earth, think about why a leader avoids a difficult conversation. The opportunity is there every day, but when you ask the leader why there was no course correction, the explanation is almost always about the inconvenience: the employee has been through a rough personal period. It's the company picnic. It's Christmas. Before you know it, ten years later, after hundreds of thousands of dollars in lost productivity due to absenteeism, low morale, and a lawsuit, we look back and say "woulda, coulda, shoulda."

Attachment

The second barrier to course correction is attachment, whether to making the numbers, to achieving a specific goal, or to the plan itself. If you remember in chapter 5 on change, attachment is one of the signs of resistance.

The major reason leaders need to declare their values is to help them make tough decisions when course correction is necessary. Too often, however, the values and vision are ignored or altered to align with the plan, instead of the plan being reworked to align with the vision and values.

When leaders view the plan as a god instead of a guide, they experience resistance to course-corrective measures. This tendency is a mind-set problem that eventually steers a leader off course and out of alignment with core values and best practices. For example, watch how often you see leaders intensely committed to staying within budget for payroll, even if that commitment comes at the expense of employee health or puts the life of an employee, patient, or client at unnecessary risk. To guard against these potentially costly and high-risk ways of thinking, leaders must understand alignment. They must embody and model the values stated as the company's core mission, so they can walk the talk and make decisions that serve the highest purpose. Sometimes you change the resources to fit the plan, and at other times you alter the plan to fit the resources. The wisdom comes in knowing which choice to make when. The problem occurs when attachment to the plan or the goal overrides alignment with higher values, or when two equal values compete, such as safety and productivity.

A Personal Story

In my decades on the factory floor at Kraft Foods, we constantly heard about the importance of safety. We had safety slogans, safety meetings, and safety award dinners when we reached one million hours with no lost-time accidents. While safety was important, it was very clear that production was too. Shutting down a line means losing money. It takes time to clear a jam out of a machine, especially when you need to push the safety lock, and then yell, "Clear" before the machine starts back up. I admit there were times when I put myself at risk to save ten seconds. The times that I did lock out the machine sometimes resulted in an angry machine operator who wanted to get his quota. I can recall numerous times getting into an argument with a machine operator when I demanded that he yell, "Clear" before I started the machine up. I was willing to risk the anger of a coworker to maintain my safety.

Unfortunately, many employees are not willing to face down social pressures to do what is necessary. Ignoring safety rules to maintain or increase productivity takes the operation a degree or two off course. The resultant higher productivity raises expectations to go even faster. Little by little, a degree at a time, the operation strays from the course—until a tragedy strikes. Then we fall back on remedial measures that would have been unnecessary if we had taken the preventive measures of regular course correction.

Leaders need to develop keen discernment to choose between two or more compelling values that do not yet align. When employees hear mixed messages that promote "safety first" but also warn, "There are consequences to pay if you don't meet productivity goals," the pressure will create a culture of high risk, which is necessary to meet the goal. Unfortunately, when an accident happens, someone usually is "held accountable" and fired for not adhering to safety rules. If it is not emotionally safe to adhere to safety rules, employees will risk their own physical safety and that of other employees as well.

Emotional Resistance

The third barrier to course correction is emotional resistance. Leaders avoid course correction for the same reason they avoid accountability: they don't want to deal with the feelings and underlying emotional issues that come with being totally responsible. Emotional resistance relates directly to the previous barrier, attachment to the plan. To admit that the plan needs to be adjusted or that there was a miscalculation in the budget requires admitting a mistake, acknowledging that you were wrong.

Leaders dislike feeling vulnerable and often do not like to admit their mistakes. This avoidance is an error with two roots: fear and the need to be perfect. Sometimes the fear is of being judged and at other times it is fear of hurting someone's feelings. **The less comfortable a leader is with dealing with her fears, the more likely she is to avoid both accountability and course correction.**

No matter what the fear, whether it's the fear of speaking up, admitting failure, losing face, or losing the race, the third barrier is all about avoiding emotions.

In aviation, there's a mathematical rule called the one in sixty rule. If you travel sixty miles in an hour you are traveling one mile per minute. If you are one tiny degree off course during that hour of travel time, you will end up one mile from your intended route. Larry Baum, president and CEO of the Computing Center in Ithaca, New York, has been flying for more than forty years and likens what he has learned from flying to running a business: "When you fly, you are in a state of constant reevaluation. You know your end result—where you want to go, but you also have to take into account the weather and how you are feeling that day. There are some pilots who will fly no matter what the weather, and those are the pilots who never get old."[2] The ones who change their plans to accommodate the realities of the weather live longer.

Making friends with reality is as important in business as it is in piloting a plane. "You want to think of the long term, not the short term," Baum said. Pilots continually seek information that alerts them to potential dangers and they must accurately assess current reality to see where they are in relation to their final destination.

What can we learn from navigation as it applies to leadership? On a macro level, correcting at 3 degrees is vastly different from course correcting at 180 degrees. While planning and prevention are keys to good decision making, there are always outside elements that have the power to alter the outcome of even the best-laid plans. Constant minor course correction takes away the drama of most situations, whether it's managing the company, leading others, or living your best life. When the leader is aware of the minor shifts that must take place to maintain alignment and course-corrects continuously, the effects are barely noticed. Most of the time, we learn about or witness the process of course correction in the drama spotlight—after the security breach, after the tragic accident, after the discovery that the budget was mismanaged.

The Renaissance Project

On January 18, 2005, William Boettcher, former CEO of Fletcher Allen Health Care in Burlington, Vermont, pleaded guilty to fraud.[3] He confessed that he had covered up the true costs of an expansion known as the Renaissance Project, which included a new emergency room, birthing center, parking garage, and ambulatory center for the area's largest nonprofit regional community hospital, serving more than one million patients throughout Vermont and northern

New York. Boettcher told the state regulators who control hospital spending that the project would cost $173 million when the true cost was $367 million. The management team maintained two sets of accounts that allowed them to keep the real financials a secret.

At first, it was believed Boettcher concealed information from the board of trustees and other executives. However, in August 2006, David Cox, former CFO, pleaded guilty to charges and admitted his role in the controversy. Eventually eight Fletcher Allen trustees resigned. The consequences for the deception were costly: Fletcher Allen was fined $1 million, and William Boettcher agreed to personally repay more than $733,000. In addition, the scandal maxed out the borrowing capacity of the hospital and inhibited its ability to borrow money to make other needed improvements.

At what point did things start veering off course? Where was the opportunity to course-correct? I would wager that attachment became a barrier. The desire to achieve the result became so compelling that an entire team was willing to let go of alignment and accountability to manifest their vision into physical reality. We may never know the reasons behind this type of conspiracy. How did it go unnoticed? Why did several leaders agree to misrepresent the facts by keeping fraudulent records with the intention of hiding financial information? Most of us read about scandals that make it to the national news believing this could never have happened if we had been on the board.

Making It Personal

It's easy to pass judgment on the Fletcher Allen executives and board members who committed fraud, but step back and ask yourself if you believe any of these individuals began with an intent to commit a crime the day they were hired. What happened that enabled this number of individuals to veer off course to such a degree that wrong decisions made over and over turned into deception and conspiracy?

Again, we can learn from these examples by looking deeply within to see how even on minor issues we all do similar things. We allow some small error once, then twice. We cover up one mistake, which leads to another cover-up. We justify the decisions along the way until what seemed like minor errors in judgment become front-page news, resulting in a firing or a lawsuit. This is why, at its core, leadership is always about character and alignment. Business skills or acumen without these core guidance components leave the door open for major errors in judgment. What we do know is that once the ship has veered 180 degrees off course, it takes more effort to turn the ship around, and in the world of business that often means a new leader.

Dr. Melinda Estes was hired to course-correct both the budget and the culture at Fletcher Allen Health Care. According to an article in *Vermont Woman*, Estes was hired not only because she was a physician with business experience but because of the "absolute clarity of answers she provided."[4] Under Estes's leadership, Fletcher Allen not only balanced its budget and paid for the expansion, it became a national example of values alignment by implementing sustainable food and health-care practices throughout its system.[5]

The Power of Conscious Course Correction

The Fletcher Allen case study provides a snapshot of how clarity, course correction, and alignment to values work together. In the YouTube video *Healthy Food in Healthcare Workshop*, Estes says, "Our success is not by accident but results from a conscious decision about the way we do things."[6]

Alignment to that commitment meant joining the Vermont Fresh Network, an organization that provides opportunities for farmers, chefs, and food producers to collaborate. The clear purpose is to improve the health of the patient. According to Estes in the video, "It starts with what you put in your mouth and how you approach diet and nutrition. As a health-care organization and an academic medical center, we have a responsibility to be leaders and models in this area."[7]

Leaders have a responsibility to make good decisions. All decisions, whether conscious or unconscious, have a ripple effect. Conscious decisions have the power to transform a culture. The transformation of Fletcher Allen not only benefits patients but also the local farmers, the community, other health-care providers, the local economy, and even the cost of health care as a whole. The health-care system supplies more than 1.5 million meals per day purchased from more than thirty local farmers. The result: the farmers have a secure income each year; patients eat fresh, healthy foods known to improve health; and the system reaps potential reductions in health-care costs. "It's important to note that, whether we pay for eating healthy today or pay for care for a patient with chronic disease later on, either way the health-care system bears those costs. Doing something right does not have to be more costly,"[8] Estes said.

Course Correction in the Trenches

Most leaders are not CEOs, trustees of a major corporation, or top executives. Most leadership roles in the workplace belong to small business owners, middle-level managers, and first-line supervisors. If we fail to recognize these individuals as leaders, we do a disservice both to the individuals in the trenches and to all companies that need to develop their leaders. Most frontline leaders such as supervisors and managers never face a major course-correction initiative like the one as Melinda Estes encountered. However, all leaders must learn how to initiate difficult conversations, set up accountability measures, and initiate unpopular changes. These course-correcting skills in the trenches help maintain alignment at every level. The act of learning is ultimately about making minor course corrections.

There is a downside to becoming excellent at making minor course corrections, however. Your efforts may barely be noticed!

Whether your course correction is in how you communicate with your employees or how you maintain your health, if you are really good at course correction, people looking in from the outside will marvel at your "luck." If they pay attention at all, that is.

Here's why: learning how to course-correct effectively takes away the hero's journey we all love. We get excited about the individual who avoided the scales for five years until his health broke under the weight he was carrying. Then when he gets invited to participate on *The Biggest Loser,* we watch his struggles after years of being off course, and we cheer him on toward his goal. It's thrilling to witness the result when finally the contestant has lost three hundred pounds, dealt with his emotional issues, and triumphed over the struggle to maintain good health habits. The reality is, if the person had course-corrected after gaining the first twenty-five pounds, there would have been very little drama.

One Thing You Cannot Delegate

Once you accept the role of leadership, the lifelong journey of self-awareness, learning, and growth begins. Part of that journey is learning how to course-correct quickly. As a leader, you can delegate many things: you can have an assistant return your calls; you can delegate the sales function; you can assign the follow-through; and you can hire others to supervise. But there is one thing no one else can do for you, and that is your inner work. The leadership journey is a state of *being* as much as it is a state of *doing*, and that will always include constant self-evaluation and course correction.

Becoming the best version of yourself requires that you constantly learn new skills, examine your beliefs, and evaluate your attitudes and behaviors. If you are diligent, you will always find room for improvement if you are willing and able to make course corrections. This requires that you see course correction as evidence you have a growth mind-set—a competitive advantage for your company. As Quaker William Penn said, "No man can master another who has not mastered himself." It is easier to help others course-correct when you have a growth mind-set, when you have put forth your best efforts and know that others are equally capable.

Helping Others Course-Correct

One of the biggest complaints I hear from supervisors and managers—those leaders in the trenches—is that an employee is not performing. What is most surprising is when I find out the problem has gone on for years without any effort on the part of the leader to give appropriate feedback or to help the employee improve her performance.

Possibly, the reason so many difficult performance conversations never take place is that the invitation to correct someone else's course never comes at a convenient time. Sometimes, the problem is that the leader doesn't want to deal with the emotions that emerge during these types of conversations. Perhaps the leader is attached to being right about how he perceives the employee rather than offering coaching to help the employee improve performance.

Another reason leaders have a difficult time course-correcting others is that they lack development in this area. The lack of leadership development always affects the level of accountability: you can't correct what you refuse to see and don't acknowledge. This inability to have a difficult conversation starts to chip away at the culture. When middle managers deny the problems, they contribute to a culture of avoidance rather than a culture of improvement. To address this problem, I have developed a process any leader can use to prepare for difficult conversations. Using this process will enable a leader to clearly articulate the needed change, measure the results, and make a decision that is aligned with the stated values.

The Importance of Clarity

As a leader, the first step in course-correcting others is to get clear about your intention. Your intention should be to help the employee, not to seek revenge. From the employee's perspective, the invitation to "talk to the boss" can be perceived as a threat. People are either in growth mode or protection mode. Your demeanor will help to create the right environment for growth. There is some work to be done before talking with the employee. Answer these three questions to attain your own clarity:

1. "What is the employee doing that he should not be doing?"
2. "What should the employee be doing that he is not doing?"
3. "How have I contributed to this problem?"

If the leader cannot answer all three of these questions in one paragraph or less, the problem is that the leader is unclear. A lack of clarity shows up in almost all business problems, including the leader not knowing what he wants from employees and employees complaining without knowing exactly what it is that the manager wants.

In fact, test me on this idea. The next time you hear someone complaining, start by listening carefully and acknowledging her frustration. Then ask, in a patient and interested tone, "Ultimately, what do you want to happen?" You will hear stories of how Sally is at fault, why what they want won't happen, and so on, until you are pulled into distraction.

Know this: lack of clarity is always going to cause drama, especially when it comes to improving employee performance. If the leader isn't clear, no amount of communication or accountability measures will help. So the three questions above should be completed before you initiate any corrective conversation with an employee. If the problem has gone on for a long time, the lack of course correction is causing the biggest problem and is affecting the culture.

To recap: analyze the observable behaviors by asking, "What is not happening that should be?" "What is happening that should not be?" and "How have I, the leader, contributed to the problem?"

Determining the Issues

Once the leader is clear about her intentions, it's time to check in to see if the employee is clear. The second part of the process includes determining what other issues contribute to the problem. Does the employee understand his job? Is there a job description? What has changed that might muddy his clarity? Have his priorities been delineated clearly? If not, you may need to improve your communication.

The next part of the process is making friends with reality. The reality could be that the employee does not have the necessary skills. Perhaps when this employee was hired, the trainer was absent and the employee was thrown into the position with little or no training.

As you can see, this type of questioning takes the drama and emotion out of the equation and helps you determine what the real issue is. If the employee is clear about her job and has the necessary skills, explore whether the real issue is a lack of resources. What equipment, knowledge, or help is needed that is not being given? These questions are based on reality rather than on assumptions about the lack of performance, and help you to know if you need to course-correct the expectations, the resources, or the employee. Does the employee understand the priority? Or is the employee simply not willing to do the job? As a leader, you can course-correct almost any issue except this last one. Unless the employee is willing, nothing happens.

Resistance, blame, or excuses all point to a negative answer to the question, "Are you willing?" If the answer is "No" and you have done due diligence, this conversation will help both you and the employee decide how to terminate the relationship with no regrets and a minimum of drama.

Leadership Influence

Understanding how to implement the process of course correction increases a leader's influence, which enables the organization to do more good in the world. Eventually, the leader's influence has the capacity to transform not only the workplace but the community, the country, and the world at large.

What is the distinction between course correction and change? The answer is perspective. When *you* are the one leading, what you view as course correction, your employees view as change. When course correction is thrust upon you from above, you will experience the course correction as a change.

Executive Summary

➢ Small course corrections take away the need for a hero to step in.
➢ Sometimes you alter the resources to fit the plan, while at other times you alter the plan.
➢ Inconvenience, attachment, and emotional resistance are barriers to course correction.
➢ Course-correcting self and others is a necessary part of leadership.

Wisdom Exercises

1. Name one to three things within your area of influence that need some minor course correction.
2. Describe your biggest obstacle to helping others course-correct.
3. Find a news article like the Fletcher Allen story and try to relate to the story from a more personal level to discern the lessons that apply.

PART 3

The Power to Create

Those who spend their lives destructively are not in touch with their power to create.

—Robert Fritz

Twenty-one-year-old Moritz Erhardt was found dead in his apartment from an epileptic seizure after working three days around the clock. As an intern at Merrill Lynch's London office, Moritz was determined to prove his worth. In the last three days of his life, he had been pulling what is known in banking circles as "a magic roundabout"—you work until 5:00 a.m. and catch a cab home to shower while the taxi waits to return you immediately to work.

Peer pressure, competition, and long hours are sometimes part of the culture in which interns and young staffers alike compete for success. After Moritz's death, the bank launched a review of work practices. An expert was quoted as saying, "We have found that working anything more than seventy hours a week is counterproductive." Conversations erupted about the competitive nature of interns and the need to make new policies to make sure the same thing didn't happen again.[1]

The issue here is not how many hours you work or your position on the workplace totem pole. Nor is it about policies to prevent interns from working too many hours. The real issues are values, culture, and the way we define success. As long as success is defined as *having* more instead of *being* more, we will continue to have workplace cultures that push for profits without considering people, encourage work without rest, and give rise to power without responsibility. As long as the workplace culture promotes internal competition over collaboration, we will continue to see toxic work environments. As long as we value clawing our way to the top more than expressing our gifts through our work, we will see more burnout and less engagement.

Change is on the horizon. Most recently, the partnership of business mogul Arianna Huffington partnered with spiritual leader Eckhart Tolle to speak about a third metric of success that consists of wisdom, well-being, wonder, and contribution. After Huffington suffered a health crisis due to overwork, she used her life lesson to share with the world: there's more to success than money: sleep is important; happiness matters.[2] Many have known these truths all along but failed to live them and got caught up in the rat race. It took a highly visible, highly successful woman who almost died from overwork to deliver the message that could be heard by the masses.

While searching for external power or criticizing the powers that be, we have forgotten about the power always available: the power to create. Creating is different from problem solving. As long as there is a problem to focus on, we spend time and resources making new policies and fixing what is broken. As long as there is a problem that has *been* fixed, there will emerge in its place yet another problem to *be* fixed.

Creating is about bringing something into existence that has not yet been. Enlightened leaders create the right environment—a culture where people are engaged and empowered, where they recognize their own power to create.

CHAPTER 7

Environment

Molecules like people, prefer environments that offer them stability.

—Bruce Lipton

Juan was concerned about a consolidation that included combining two groups of public safety telecommunicators into one agency. The twenty employees working in Agency A would all lose their jobs and have to reapply to join the thirty-two employees in Agency B.[1] Agency B employees would have to endure others coming into their territory and disrupting their happy family. Both Agency A and Agency B employees would have to learn new rules and new ways of working together. From Juan's perspective and past experience, it wasn't going to be easy.

While the decision to consolidate belonged to the leaders of city government, dealing with the human side belonged to Juan. He dreaded the emotional reactions that almost always come with unwanted change: from turf wars and tattling to arguments about the way things have always been done to debates about seniority. Juan, stuck between the city leaders and the people he had to lead, took a deep breath and prepared a memo inviting everyone to a meeting.

Culture clash is the main reason for unnecessary drama in

mergers, acquisitions, or consolidations. What leaders often forget is that what looks good on paper often does not work out the way they'd thought. Reality includes human beings. Human beings come with preferences, assumptions, beliefs, and emotions, all of which create resistance during periods of unwanted change.

Groups of human beings come with shared language, histories, and norms, none of which can be accurately translated onto a spreadsheet to predict the success or failure of a change effort. If people were robots, an analytical leader could simply look at the numbers on a spreadsheet and move some things around to control the outcome. The leader would only have to be concerned with product and process.

Enlightened leaders understand that it's the people who make the processes work. A team that works together when things are running smoothly may not be able to perform when influences from outside the environment pose a threat to the status quo.

Leaders influence environment, and environment influences culture. Enlightened leaders do not try to change the culture. Instead, they use their power to create the environment that will produce the desired results.

Culture

Culture is a topic that some avoid discussing because it seems either overwhelming or unimportant. Culture is often defined as a set of beliefs that govern behavior, alternately defined as "the way we do things around here." Dr. Edgar Schein, whom we talked about in chapter 5, is one of the top thought leaders on culture. He told me, "Culture is what a group learns as its way of surviving and both getting along internally and solving its problems externally."[2] Schein said what's usually missing is an understanding of how the external environment influences culture.

Let's turn our attention to the differences between culture and environment and to the ways leaders intentionally and unintentionally influence the environment. Whether they are aware of it or not, leaders have the power to shape or even transform culture in the workplace.

All workplace cultures are subcultures of other, larger systems. For example, there is the culture of the country in which you live, but there is also the culture of the state, county, town, and so on, and there is your company culture. The company you work for is a subculture of an industry such as manufacturing, public safety, banking, health care, or education. History, geographical location, climate, legislation, competition, and leadership are some of the environmental influences on the culture of an organization. In short, there are reasons for the way we do things around here, and there are reasons for the beliefs that govern behavior in any workplace. The challenge is in understanding which influences are at play and how the internal and external environment can be co-created or altered.

The best place to start understanding culture is to look at your own. We all see the world through the lens of our own experiences. From this self-examination, we begin to understand the significance of culture and how culture influences thinking and behaviors. Where you were born, the type of family you were raised in, the language you speak, and where you have worked are all smaller cultures that are part of *the* culture in which you live and work. Enlightened leaders use this knowledge to understand self and others, so that they can get results and minimize drama.

Internal Environment

When people talk about workplace culture, they are usually referring to the internal environment. The internal environment comprises groups of people who interact to offer a product or service to customers. Groups need to learn to work together in the inside environment so they can offer products and services to their clients in the outside environment.

When employees join an organization, they quickly learn the rules of the game and what it takes to blend in. They learn how to survive and get along inside the workplace. Employees learn to disengage when their ideas are not listened to. They learn to tattle and gossip if they can get the ear of their supervisor. Employees learn what they can get by with and what they can't. If the leader turns a blind eye to misbehavior, employees take liberties. In the internal environment, leaders have the greatest ability to effect change in people's behavior.

The internal environment also consists of the building, lighting, furniture, equipment, and space. Physical space and equipment can significantly alter behavior. Remember, in chapter 5, I talked about how people in the plant bickered and argued over a chair? Simply providing a couple of new chairs would probably have helped people get a long a little better. When employees do not have enough resources to comfortably do their jobs, internal competitiveness negatively shapes the culture. Later, I'll share an example of how one enlightened leader transformed a wine store by working with the visible internal environment.

The External Environment

Workplace culture is also shaped by the external environment. The external environment includes customers, competitors, legislators, new technology, and any change from the external that could benefit or threaten the company.

Here is a snapshot of a St. Louis company and how the external environment influenced and shaped the culture. Barry-Wehmiller started in 1885 as a machine shop that provided conveying and transportation equipment to malt houses. Soon the product line expanded to include machines that washed reusable bottles. These external changes to the product line no doubt created changes to the internal environment.[3]

Other changes within the internal environment came about

as the ownership shifted from the Wehmiller family to the Chapman family. When Bill Chapman died suddenly of a heart attack in 1976, his son, Bob Chapman, became chairman and CEO. What Chapman could have not predicted was the external change about to take place that would test his leadership abilities.

Anheuser-Busch depended upon Barry-Wehmiller as a supplier just as Barry-Wehmiller depended upon Anheuser-Busch's business. Anheuser-Busch, a client since 1901, had become one of Barry-Wehmiller's biggest customers, providing predictable revenues each year. When Anheuser-Busch's senior vice president, who had built a relationship with the Chapman family, retired, the new vice president decided to change suppliers, putting a tremendous strain on the company.

This external environmental change altered Chapman's direction and leadership: he decided to never again rely on just one customer, one market, or one technology. As a result, Chapman began diversifying and growing Barry-Wehmiller through acquisitions. Over the course of many years, and many challenges, the company completely transformed under Bob Chapman's leadership. In 2014, *Inc.* magazine named Barry-Wehmiller one of its "Most Audacious Companies" in the area of culture. Stay tuned, and I will fill in the gaps that got the company from struggling and stumbling to walking the talk.

Understanding culture, the differences between internal and external environments, and how culture is shaped by environment is even more important for leaders working in the global economy of the twenty-first century.

Environment As Scaffolding

One of the most brilliant definitions I have heard so far comes from my friend and consulting colleague, Aviv Shahar, a world leader in strategic innovation, who said, "Environment is the scaffolding on which culture hangs."[4] Aviv helps senior executives create new futures. When I spoke with him, he said he has never facilitated a meeting where he didn't need to work with the environment to create the outcome he wanted. Aviv said leaders need to understand they have the power to create or cocreate the environment.

Let's build the scaffolding. Figure 7.1 shows the Cultural Framework Model, or CFM for short. Notice the two solid horizontal lines and two vertical dashed lines. The solid horizontal lines represent the visible elements of the internal and external environment. The two vertical dashed vertical lines represent the invisible elements of the internal and external environment.

Together these four elements create the scaffolding on which culture hangs. See Figure 7.1 and notice it looks like a tic-tac-toe board with culture hanging in the middle.

Now it's easy to see, as illustrated in Figures 7.2 and 7.3, that when a change occurs in the visible or invisible, in the external or internal, the shape of the scaffolding changes, and in doing so, affects the culture.

Culture hangs in the middle.

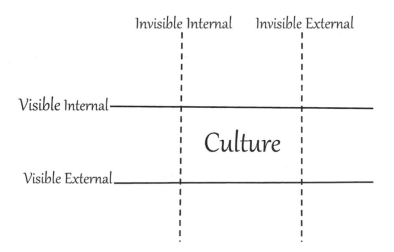

Figure 7-1: Cultural Framework Model

The Invisible Internal

The invisible elements of the internal environment represented by the dashed lines include the history, processes, tacit assumptions, attitudes, and beliefs that eventually manifest into the physical realm of behaviors and *"the way we do things around here."*

We have so much trouble with the invisible that we use words to talk about it, to make what we are seeing as tangible as possible.

My friend and fellow consultant Martyn Drake, founder of Binley Drake Consulting, based in the United Kingdom, shared his thoughts: "Companies often have internal barriers between departments that they refer to as silos. We all know the word silo is a metaphor—there are no physical silos anywhere to be seen, but it's actually a really unhelpful metaphor. In reality, it's a convenient way to avoid the truth about what's going wrong. If we told the truth, we'd say there is a lack of communication and cooperation between our departments, between your people and mine, between you and me. That's the honesty we need, if we want to find solutions."[5]

Drake's approach, like my own, is to get the individuals to take personal responsibility rather than seeing the problem as a shared function:

> You have to shift your mind-set and see these silos for what they really are—they're relationships. Your relationships. And they aren't working. If you want the relationship to change, you have to start with the part that you control, which is your own behavior. You can't dismantle silos because you can't fix something that isn't real. What you can do is take responsibility for your thoughts and your mind-set, for what you say and what you do. You can take ownership of your relationships. And you can take personal responsibility for making them work.[6]

123

Not addressing the invisible components is a potentially dangerous oversight. Enlightened leaders understand that anything visible was once invisible. The physical was once nonphysical. Our relationships are mostly invisible. The majority of your relationships with other people involve how you think about them in their absence and how you process information about them when you are with them. The stories you tell yourself about the people in your life affect your relationship with them.

If this sounds too woo-woo, take a breath and consider this fact: for anything to come into physical form, there must have been a thought or a desire. For example, Jack Stack, of SRC whom I spoke about in chapter 4, had the thought, "Why don't we try to buy this place?" First came a desire, then the idea eventually manifested into action. The actions included seeking investors and securing a loan. This realm of the invisible transformed an entire culture and became part of the history of both SRC and The Great Game of Business. This is an example of how the leader's mindset and ideas become the guiding force in the invisible internal environment.

The Invisible External

The invisible external as represented in Figure 7.1 includes regulations, laws, and ideas from the outside. These invisible forces, such as new legislation, or regulatory changes can dramatically alter your business or the leader's decision making. Any new law has the capacity to alter your business dramatically. The variable that can change your plans and push you into unwanted change is invisible external environmental forces.

When legislation passed that allowed the Centers for Medicare and Medicaid Services (CMS) to penalize health-care organizations that didn't convert to electronic records management, large hospitals and small clinics alike were practically forced to comply.

The HITECH program empowered CMS to offer incentives for meaningful use of electronic health-care records, including bonuses for a few years for providers who complied, then penalties through reduced Medicare/Medicaid reimbursement for those who didn't comply in the following years.

No matter how great the teamwork was, even the best of teams sometimes found it difficult to work together under the stress that comes with learning new technology, purging files, and finding new ways to get along on the inside and survive on the outside.

Express Employment Professionals produced a white paper, *The Growing Impact of Wage-and-Hour Regulations,*[7] that said nearly 56 percent of companies had been involved in lawsuits about employee exemption, all due to state and federal regulatory changes. The laws fluctuate and change so rapidly that most leaders are challenged to keep up. According to Fox News, in an article entitled "Regulation Nation: Drowning in Rules, Businesses Brace for Cost and Time for Compliance," "regulations rose to 3,573 final rules in 2010, up from 3,503 in 2009, the equivalent of about 10 per week."

These changes, initiated by the state and federal government happen outside of the company's control, yet the changes always affect the company culture and how the company leaders make decisions. For example, "Businesses are switching employees from salaried to hourly. IBM reclassified 7,000 employees to hourly, resulting in a 15 percent cut to the worker's salary to allow for possible overtime."[8] Influences from the outside trickle into how companies make decisions to survive, and in turn, those decisions affect the culture on the inside.

The Profit and Amazing Grapes

Let me share an example of how changes to the internal visible environment, along with the leader's intention and knowledge, transformed a company in Orange County, California. *The Profit,* a show on CNBC, illustrates how successful businessman and investor

Marcus Lemonis saves family businesses using his own money and expertise. Lemonis said about the series, "My only interest is people, process, and product."[9] Over and over again, he confirms that the reason a business fails or succeeds is because of people.

On one particular episode, Lemonis worked with Amazing Grapes, a wine bar and retail store that was losing money. The highest margin for the business was the bar, yet the bar was located in a small corner at the back of the building, while the walk-in retail area was taking up most of the space. Lemonis decided to change the inner visible environment to increase margins. He renovated the inside of the building, bringing the bar front and center. He eliminated clutter and the aisles of wine racks, and replaced the surrounding walls with artistic wine racks to display the wine. Expanded seating provided more space for customers to order food and peruse the selection of wine for purchase, which was displayed beautifully along the walls.

This intentional change allowed Amazing Grapes to capitalize on the square footage and drive more sales. The processes (internal environmental changes) enabled people to work more efficiently, and the new use of space and the beautiful design allowed the bar and restaurant business to expand. The external visible environment responded to the changes of the internal environment: more customers came to enjoy and purchase wine, and, subsequently, margins increased dramatically.

It's easy to forget that all of the changes at Amazing Grapes started in the invisible internal environment: Through Lemonis's ideas, knowledge, and leadership. His intention to transform the company not only improved sales, it increased employee engagement. Through regular meetings, employees were updated and involved in the business. Lemonis even gave the employees some shares of ownership, which altered the invisible realm—the employees' attitudes and commitment. Look at figure 7.3 to see a visual representation of how the internal invisible eventually shaped both the visible internal and external environment. The

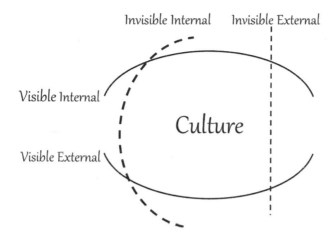

Figure 7-2: Culture Framework Model

only environmental element that was unchanged was the invisible external.

Leaders can and do influence the environment either consciously or unconsciously. Even where there is no budget to renovate a building, minor changes can increase productivity; at the least, small improvements can promote pride in the company. Simply changing the lighting, providing quiet places for those who need to concentrate, or simply keeping the lobby clear of clutter can improve workplace relationships and increase efficiency.

Acts of God

No matter how much planning you do and how much cooperation you get, forces like the weather and other unforeseen incidents, referred to as "acts of God," can and will change your plans and results. These acts of God are what I refer to in chapter 5, on change, as Quadrant 4: change that was unexpected and unwanted. Acts of God across the globe include earthquakes, tsunamis, tornados, floods, and fires. Large or small, any act of God is a change in the external environment that changes plans and alters behaviors.

I was preparing for a seminar for thirty invitation-only participants. I'd rented an expensive ballroom on the top floor of an office complex overlooking the city. I had the waitstaff arrange the tables to fit the environment, and I made sure the lighting, the décor, and all components worked to create an intimate space conducive to conversation and learning.

From experience, I have learned that if the room is too large, you lose intimacy, and if the temperature is too hot or cold, people will be uncomfortable and unable to focus. Knowing that food distracts, I ordered a buffet lunch and set aside enough time to enjoy it. These are all examples of working with the visible internal environment to produce a desired outcome.

When participants arrived, I set the expectations for the day, eliminating for attendees the possible distractions of wondering when they'd be able to check cell phones or whether it was a good time to run to the restroom. This is an example of working with the invisible environmental influences to help create structure.

In the workplace, the rules and policies of a company are the internal invisible structures that shape how we do things and how people get along. When rules and policies are in place but are not enforced, drama follows.

In my situation, setting up participants' expectations encourages their participation and discourages distractions. After all this preparation, five minutes before the seminar was to start, a tornado warning erupted and sent all of the participants, including myself, down to the basement with about one thousand other scared individuals from surrounding offices. The eight-hour retreat that was promised turned into a three-hour retreat minus thirty minutes for lunch. See the Culture Framework Model, Figure 7-3. This is an example of how the external shapes the environment. Leaders must prepare to adjust accordingly to continue to provide value. When any one of the four elements change, the other elements adjust and evolve to shift the way we do things and the beliefs and behaviors.

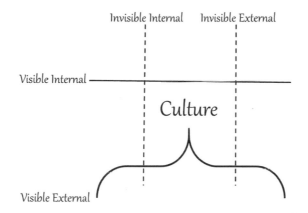

Figure 7-3: Culture Framework Model

Behavior is influenced by the culture, and in the Midwest, the culture is to take cover when there's a tornado warning!

Imagine how this understanding of how to interact and cocreate with the environment could increase learning in classrooms and facilitate heightened levels of engagement. How would this understanding change the way leaders make decisions or manage change?

Let's revisit the situation of Juan, the manager of public safety telecommunicators: the changes both agencies face stems from the outside environment. The outside environment in this case is the decision made by government leaders. This decision will affect all of the individuals in both agencies and will be a determining factor in creating a new culture. The internal chaos inside the environment will contribute to a new history, which will lead to new beliefs and assumptions about what it means to consolidate. These experiences will contribute to beliefs not only in the small combined culture but also in the industry as a whole. The unenlightened leader sees problems to be solved, while the enlightened leader sees an opportunity to work with the environment to create something new.

How Leaders Affect Environment

The path of least resistance when drama erupts is to either cast blame or to look for ways to change the culture. A better alternative is to look at the business problem and consider ways you can change the environment.

Remember the example in chapter 5, when employees fought over a chair when there weren't enough? Most leaders look at these issues as arising from bad employee morale or workplace drama. You can send the bickering employees to a conflict management seminar, or you can change the environment by ordering a few new chairs. Employees can be difficult, no doubt. But, when the fingers start pointing, it's always an indicator that it's also time to look at the environment and leadership. Let me share another "chair" story from my factory days.

In my early days at Kraft Foods, I was transferred to the new pasta plant. My only job was to watch the product fly down the lines and pick off any rejects. If there was a problem that produced waste, my job was to "peel out" the substandard product into a steel bin. If there was a really big mess, my job was to sweep the floor.

The business unit manager, I'll call him Howard, was well liked but known to be a workaholic. Howard was there at almost every shift, and everyone wondered if he ever slept. The problem was, he thought everyone should be as driven as he was. Therefore, he did not believe that anyone in the department should have a chair. As a result, anytime the coast was clear, we worker bees would try to "sneak a sit" on the table used for weighing the product. When he came walking through the department, people would swiftly jump off of the table and commence sweeping the floor, going with the philosophy, "If you've got time to lean, you've got time to clean."

It's easy to look at this and laugh at the absurdity of it all. When there were productivity problems, there was no time to sit anyway. When things were running smoothly, standing produced no better results than sitting. The point is that this leader, through his own belief system, created an environment where employees sneaked around to grab five minutes of relief from standing on a concrete floor for eight hours.

The choices seem obvious when looking back, but I swear I see the same kinds of minuscule problems today. Instead of rethinking a position, leaders spend extra time policing an area rather than change their minds about allowing employees to take a small break. A leader's mindset and belief systems influence the environment, and the environment influences the culture. The Leadership Impact Table below, Figure 7-4, shows ten ways leaders unknowingly contribute to a negative internal environment and what to do instead to make a positive impact.

Negative Impact	Positive Impact
Not showing up	Make yourself visible to your employees
Hiding information	Share as much information as possible
Listening to hearsay and gossip	Make each person represent himself or herself
Reward systems create competitiveness	Reward on team efforts
Taking all the credit	Acknowledge team and individual efforts
Failure to keep promises	Schedule promises in order to keep them
Multitasking while employees talk	Pay attention and be present while listening
Knee-jerk reactions and temper blow ups	Take a breath and wait until calm to correct
Avoiding difficult conversations	Provide coaching and feed-forward
Unclear direction	Regular updates and specific instructions

Figure 7-4: Leadership Impact Table

Healthy Environments Help Employees Thrive

One of my interests is to take learning from other disciplines and apply the universal lessons to business. After reading Bruce Lipton's book *The Biology of Belief*,[10] I started to understand how environments affect people. As a tenured medical professor teaching medical students at the University of Wisconsin School of Medicine, Lipton had dedicated his life to studying single cells and how they thrive. He arrived at six discoveries:

1. When the cell is ailing, first look to the environment.
2. When cells have a healthy environment, they thrive.
3. Cells actively seek environments that support their survival.
4. Cells actively seek to avoid toxic or hostile environments.
5. When cells band together, they increase their awareness.
6. The more awareness a cell has of its environment, the better its chance for survival.

The fourth discovery—that cells actively seek to avoid toxic or hostile environments—also applies to employees. People generally avoid dealing with hotheaded, unreasonable, emotionally unstable bosses, and people dread coming to work when they are not part of the "in" group or when there is a great deal of negativity and resistance. From this perspective it doesn't take a white paper to explain how toxic work environments contribute to low engagement, absenteeism, and turnover. Number 6, relating to a cell's awareness of its environment and increased survival, also applies to success in the workplace. Isn't it true that the more aware a new employee is of your organization's culture, the easier it is to onboard and integrate her? Isn't that why so many mergers fail, because the environment is hostile or there is a lack of awareness of how to band together? Isn't it also true that being aware of others is a prerequisite for solidifying the relationship and working together to meet company goals?

What Lipton taught medical students about cellular biology also applies to organizations and culture. To experiment, I've used basically the same sentence but replaced the word "cell" with either "people" or "person."

1. When the **person** is ailing, first look to the environment.
2. When **people** have a healthy environment, they thrive.
3. **People** actively seek environments that support their survival.
4. **People** actively seek to avoid toxic or hostile environments.
5. When **people** band together, they increase their awareness.

6. The more awareness a **person** has of his environment, the better his chance for survival.

Lipton had the opportunity to experience these truths when he took an assignment to teach cellular biology on a remote Caribbean island, a refreshing contrast to the university environment. His mission was to prepare medical students who had not passed the strenuous exams required for traditional medical school.

These students, driven by their desire to become doctors, had used their savings to study outside the United States in a last-ditch effort to realize their dreams. After the students failed their first exam and were told they had to repeat a semester, Lipton was determined to give everything he had to help them succeed.

Throwing away conventional methods, Lipton encouraged them to really learn the material instead of just memorizing it. He taught them to think of the cells as human beings. He planted new ideas in their heads and aided them in eliminating the assumption that they had to perform like medical students at the university: cutthroat, competitive, and single-minded. Instead, he had them work together so that the weaker students could learn from the stronger students. To quote from his book: "My class of misfits stopped acting like conventional medical students; they dropped their survival of the fittest mentality and amalgamated into a single force, a team that helped them survive the semester. The stronger students helped the weaker and, in so doing, all became stronger."[11] Lipton gave his students the same stringent exam he gave his Wisconsin students.

"There was virtually no difference in the performance of these 'rejects' and their 'elitist' counterparts in the States,"[12] he said. In addition, when the students returned home to the United States, their understanding was deeper than that of some of their fellow doctors. Lipton said, "Instead of mirroring smart American medical students, they mirrored the behavior of smart cells banding together to become smarter."[13]

Creating Healthy Environments

Many of the company leaders who have been profiled in this book align with the principles that Lipton discovered in his days of teaching cellular biology. For example, Stacey Peterson and Joe Chinn, leaders of the City of Rancho Cordova, California, told me they try to provide a workplace where there is "freedom to be you."[14] They seek to provide an environment at work that is a little piece of heaven. Employees make suggestions, and the suggestions are honored. Peterson said, "People come into an organization with talents, hobbies, and we try to capitalize on them."[15] The city has provided bikes, a vegetable garden, and a city band—three ideas employees volunteered with and implemented.

Express Employment Professionals provides education to its new franchise owners to increase the new owners' business knowledge and ensure success. Franchisees have continued support though headquarters as well as access to an annual sales summit and an international leadership conference. Express recently added Express Leadership Academy, committed to building entrepreneurial excellence.

Nikki Sells, CEO/Principal of Sells Development Inc., spent more than twenty-five years with Express, first as a franchise owner and later as the vice president of franchising at corporate headquarters. She said:

I had the great opportunity to be raised by Express, and this has contributed to my success today as a consultant to other franchisors who want to increase their sales. What I've learned, though, is that when you are actually working for the company, you may not recognize how fortunate you are to work in a particular culture, but then when you look back you see it differently. I don't know of any other company that invests the kind of resources they do on growing their internal staff. They offer opportunities, they offer classes, they are committed to leadership development and they really walk the talk.[16]

Dixon Schwabl, the advertising agency we talked about earlier, engages its team of eighty-five employees to come up with creative ideas for the company's internal environment. When the team suggested putting a waterfall inside the building, the cost was prohibitive. So instead of buying a waterfall, the company built a building around one that was already in place. As a result of the environment they have created, the company has been able to increase applications for employment by 230 percent. More than 350 people applied for the position of chief creative officer.

At SRC, employees are encouraged to come up with ideas for improving productivity. If one of those ideas is accepted, the employee is paid for the idea. The culture is such that everyone talks to everyone else, regardless of their titles or positions. Employees are taught to be entrepreneurs and armed with business knowledge that secures their future.

Earlier I noted that Bob Chapman, CEO of Barry-Wehmiller, had gone through many challenges that eventually led to the transformation of his company. Barry-Wehmiller experienced a 40 percent drop in new equipment ordering in 2009. It was this occurrence that offered Bob an opportunity to walk the talk. Referring to the company's Guiding Principles of Leadership and "measuring success by the way we touch the lives of others," the leadership decided against layoffs. [17] Instead, Chapman had an idea about sharing the sacrifice through voluntary furloughs, a temporary freeze on executive bonuses, and a short-term suspension of 401(k) matches. As we learned from Dr. Lipton earlier, both cells and people actively seek environments that support their survival.

In his article, "Walk Your Talk," on the company blog, Chapman shared the story in depth: "The furlough plan revealed that we cared deeply about our team members. They felt an overwhelming sense of relief that they could count on their jobs and income.

Furthermore, they were happy to offer up four weeks of income, knowing that it was not to make the company more profitable but rather to keep others from losing their jobs!"[18]

Culture is influenced by the environment, internal and external, visible and invisible. Where there is a lack of engagement, look at the environment and then at the leadership. Where there is a lack of empowerment, look at the environment and then at the leadership. Enlightened leaders know they have the power to create the right environment, one in which employees are engaged and empowered to work together for the good of the company.

Executive Summary

➤ The environment consists of the external and internal, the visible and invisible.
➤ Healthy environments help employees thrive.
➤ A leader's beliefs and mind-set influence the environment.
➤ All workplace cultures are subcultures of other, larger systems.

Wisdom Exercises

1. Select one item on the Negative Impact Table and commit to making an improvement over the course of one month.
2. Describe an invisible environmental influence that has shaped your culture. Is the influence internal or external?
3. Do an informal survey to ask team members for ways to improve the environment.

CHAPTER 8

Engagement

Control leads to compliance; autonomy leads to engagement.
—Daniel H. Pink

When Denise Bredfeldt, an employee for International Harvester first laid eyes on Jack Stack the new plant manager, she was hanging from a hoist in the transmission area, where the guys had hooked her up by the back of her coveralls; they'd then gone off to break, leaving her hanging. She recalled: "That wasn't the first time that had happened. This particular time just happened at a time Jack was walking through the aisle. I've said many times that had I known the true meaning of the word sexual harassment and hostile environment, I would be a very wealthy woman right now. Jack was pretty new. I'm not really sure if he even saw me, but he just walked right on by and kept on walking."[1]

Bredfeldt, a hard worker respected by the people on the floor, was an influencer—but she was also a rebel. Bredfeldt had developed an underground newsletter for employees' eyes only. The newsletter served as a way to express the frustrations she and the employees experienced.

Bredfeldt said, "My peers were brilliant in dreaming up the shenanigans. The horseplay level (although still active) decreased substantially, both in frequency and ridiculousness, when Jack got there. Before he came, we weren't very productive. After he got there, we became very productive and cost conscious. The underground newspaper was written two months before the buyout and parodied life as an employee of our uncaring corporate boss, International Harvester. Looking back, I could have easily turned it into a 1980s *Dilbert* comic strip. The buyout happened several years after Jack showed up in Springfield."

Engagement or lack thereof, is not necessarily the real issue. Employees are always engaged in something. Engagement is a matter of where employees put their interest, initiative, and involvement. Enlightened leaders take the energy and focus the energy to align with the mission, vision, and values of the company.

The Importance of Purpose

Bredfeldt and I have a few things in common. We were both line workers in a factory during the 1970s and 1980s. During some of my factory years, I also was known for publishing some underground materials—mostly funny poems and limericks about the problems of the day during a period when layoffs were imminent. Realize that these shenanigans happened before e-mail, texting, and social media. One of my poems made it into the mailroom and into the mailboxes of every single supervisor. Looking back, it's surprising that my coworkers didn't tattle on me. I could have been fired.

Instead, coworkers across the plant, and even a few supervisors and business unit managers, enjoyed the drama stirred up by the witch hunt to find out who instigated the mail. I was also involved in some pretty intense water fights and other forms of horseplay when I had to do sanitation on Friday nights. I was a good worker, but in the early years, when factory culture was a lot looser than it is today, I simply had too much energy to burn—and that energy was not always productive. Nonetheless, the rules tightened long before I left, and I'm sure the things we got by with would not be tolerated today. The point I am making is that energy can be turned around. When people find purpose, they engage in the positive direction that benefits the company. When people do not find purpose, they trade their boredom for horseplay, gossip, and other forms of workplace drama.

Engagement is the new buzzword. Companies offer engagement training and engagement initiatives, hire chief engagement officers, and produce surveys to try to figure out how to build engagement. Companies want engagement because studies show that engaged employees are more loyal, have better workplace relationships, and produce better business outcomes. As a result, leaders pursue engagement using a checklist or they launch an initiative or a scientific project in hopes of getting employees to engage and help the business thrive. The problem is, engagement is *not* a project or a checklist. It is the direct result of a symbiotic relationship in which company and employee exchange value for value. The culture of the workplace influences the definition for engagement in that culture.

Defining Engagement

Just as companies need to define leadership, they also need to define engagement as it relates to their culture. If you don't have a working definition for engagement, you won't know how to redefine engagement based on meeting employee needs or how to open up to new opportunities based on change. What works for one company would not be appropriate for another, based on their different purpose, environment, and culture. Clarity comes in defining exactly what engagement looks like inside your own company. For example, SRC's culture of teaching open-book management engages the minds of employees so they are both involved in understanding financials and encouraged to take initiative and come up with ideas that reduce costs or increase revenues.

At Dixon Schwabl, engagement occurs when teams share ideas. According to Lauren Dixon:

> Teamwork here is very, very different. In most traditional advertising agencies, in the creative department, many are very egotistical, and when someone shares an idea, it has to be their own. Here, if you walked into a brainstorming session you would never know or care, when you leave, whose idea that was because someone will toss out an idea and then somebody else will take it and twist it and tweak it and then it takes on a life of its own. Nobody really cares whose idea it is, all we care about is that we bring forth the biggest, most awesome, never-before-thought-of idea. No one is so concerned about who gets credit.[2]

When I worked the blue-collar lines in the factory, *"engagement"* as a buzzword didn't exist. However, if the word had existed, I imagine engagement would have been defined as working overtime, doing a good job, having good attendance, and perhaps joining a committee or participating in the safety slogan contest.

Most executives, managers, and consultants have very little understanding of what it's like to work on the front lines, therefore they do not have much empathy or humility. My hope is that executives, managers, and other consultants can learn from my experience. The ability to understand the viewpoints of different levels is one of the greatest gaps in leadership development. We learned years ago from Stephen Covey how to "seek first to understand," the fifth habit in his book, *The 7 Habits of Highly Effective People.* However, very few of us take the time or initiative to practice this skill. This skill deficit is part of the reason leaders fail to create the right environment for engagement.

Our ability to communicate with people at various levels within the organization is directly related to our ability to understand how individuals evolve as their needs are met. This understanding helps leaders offer opportunities to employees that create what I call "enlightened engagement."

My Story

I joined Kraft Foods right out of high school. My immediate need was security. I was an engaged employee because I got my security needs met. Later, I got some of my esteem needs met when one particular supervisor trained me on some higher-level jobs and had faith in me. Some of my coworkers engaged because they got their relationship needs met. Some of the college graduates who got hired to become supervisors or business unit managers engaged as they met their career needs. When supervisors got promoted to business unit managers, they got their status needs met, as well as an ability to use their business gifts.

Employees engage with what is valuable to them. When their workplace provides opportunities to meet their needs, employees naturally gravitate to the opportunities and get involved. Engagement is a symbiotic relationship of value for value. If the company sees the employee as a cog in a wheel, the employee sees the company as a paycheck. It's really that simple. When there are opportunities for employees to share their unique gifts or to develop other interests, they give the company their heart, mind, and soul.

However, a problem occurs when people grow. What engages an individual in the beginning ceases to engage the same individual as he progresses through his career. Daniel Pink, author of five books about business, work, and management, including *A Whole New Mind*,[3] has done some interesting research in his book *Drive: The Surprising Truth About What Motivates Us*.[4] His YouTube video talks about a research project at MIT that offered a challenge in which people had three opportunities for rewards.[5] When the task required mechanical skills, the $50 monetary reward was enough. When the task required cognitive skills, the $50 was not a motivator.

The researchers repeated the experiment in India with great incentives. The higher the reward, the worse the performance; financial incentives only work for mechanical tasks. I interpret this to mean, you might get their backs but you won't get their souls. Real workplace engagement is about passion, about sharing heart and soul. Employees engage most deeply with what interests them and what captures their intellectual curiosity, their development needs, and their desires.

When the task requires conceptual or creative thinking, financial incentives and carrot-and-stick motivators simply do not work to entice people to go above and beyond. All things considered, when the money is sufficient and security needs are met, the three factors that lead to better performance are autonomy, mastery, and purpose. For the purpose of employee engagement, self-direction is better than mandates from supervisors or upper management. People want to get better at what they do, and they want to find purpose in their work. It's not all about the money. My own story bears witness to these truths.

As I was finishing my college degree, I knew I had more to offer—I could do more than work on the lines, stack skids, weigh product, and clean equipment. I had a burning desire to discover, develop, and deliver my gifts to the workplace. The advice I received at college was to start where I was, so I started looking for opportunity right in my workplace. There were opportunities to join steering committees and other initiatives. As much as I tried, nothing inspired me, and as a result I was not engaged.

Eventually, an opportunity to present a safety program got my attention, and *not* because of my love for safety. Anyone who has ever had to attend an OSHA safety class knows they are anything but enlightening; safety meetings are boring but mandatory. I was interested because of the opportunity to use my creative skills; I wanted to make something boring into something interesting, and to improve my presentation skills. I volunteered to do the training, which consisted of showing the proper ways to use chemicals, explaining why we need to wear safety goggles and earplugs, and demonstrating the proper way to wear protective gear during sanitation.

I asked management if I could be creative in making the presentation. I got their support, and I set up the program to include quizzes, role-plays, and colorful slides. I asked if I could get some product (macaroni and cheese) and some T-shirts to give away for prizes when people engaged. Management said yes. As a side note, I want to say that it's risky sometimes for frontline people to get engaged at this level. You put yourself at risk for being called a "brownnoser" or getting ridiculed for "sucking up to management." But I was ready and I understood the risk.

To my surprise, after the safety presentation, I got rave reviews. Even people who didn't necessarily like me told me it was the best safety program they had ever attended. I was elated. Then my balloon deflated. I received no acknowledgement from my boss or any of upper management. They barely noticed. To them, the presentation was simply an item on the checklist to be checked off: Meeting date set. Check. Room Reserved. Check. Notices sent. Check. Sign-in list available. Check. Volunteer presenter. Check. The end.

Speaking in terms of Daniel Pink's discovery, I got the chance to work on something and to put my creative efforts to use. I explored **autonomy**. Doing a presentation allowed me the chance to get better at something I was already interested in. I achieved some **mastery**. I had yet to discover the **purpose** part; however, I now see that this incident gave me the insight to move from the factory floor toward a new purpose.

What I do know from that experience is that by offering some leadership development, companies can build the structures and environment in which employees can discover autonomy, mastery, and purpose. Unfortunately, most employees do not know how to articulate their needs. Nor do they have the capacity to tell their employers what would most effectively stimulate their motivation and engagement. But I can, so I will, because I've been there.

What Employees Won't Tell You

This is what companies and even frontline leaders do not understand: those employees in the trenches want you to notice them. They want to do a good job. They want to be respected. They will engage if the right opportunity and the right fit presents itself. Many employees on the front lines, and in jobs like factory work, housekeeping, and nurses' aides, start their jobs only to meet financial needs. The reason they do not grow—the reason they do not pour their heart and soul into the work—is that the cultural framework does not support them doing so. In addition, many come from backgrounds and family histories that are all about survival rather than vision, choice, and personal development.

One of the biggest opportunities missed by companies everywhere is tapping into the power already present within their system. They miss the opportunity to create something magnificent when they fail to learn about—and care about—the needs of frontline employees. The key is developing the frontline supervisors and managers to become leaders, so that they can in turn develop the eyes to see the potential in the employees they lead. In a nutshell, the answer lies in opportunity and development.

As a frontline employee, my greatest desire was to be encouraged and to open the door for future opportunities, but the factory culture simply did not support that need. Leaders can use the power of cultural awareness to pay attention to what makes employees excited and what makes them complain. There you will find opportunities to increase engagement. (I'll say more about the complaining aspect later.)

After my presentation had gone unremarked upon, I felt a door had been closed, but I decided to stretch and continue to do everything I could. I set up a meeting with the plant manager. We had always heard that upper management maintained an open-door policy and invited us to come in to talk about anything. So I decided to test it out. I walked in and said to the plant manager, "I want something more and don't know how to make that happen here."

He rolled his chair back and assumed the prayer-hands position as he tried to figure out what in the heck I was talking about. "Go on," he said, looking perplexed.

"I am good at teaching," I said. "I'm good at training and development. I know how to motivate people who work here. I would love to find a way to use these skills but I don't know how. Can you help me to figure it out?"

The only thing he said was, "What is your credibility? What gives you the right to step into that kind of position here?"

I didn't know what to say. What I heard was, "You aren't enough." I felt demeaned and defeated.

Crossing Cultural Boundaries

My plant manager was not a bad person, and I was not a bad employee. Much of this issue boils down to the culture of factory life and the culture of hierarchy in manufacturing—the history of who we are, what we believe, how we do things, what is appropriate, and what is possible regarding the various roles and points of view. Edgar Schein, the former MIT Sloan professor I've referred to previously, said to me, "We don't encourage the bottom because they're at the bottom. Your plant manager had no insight into potential, not because he was a bad human being but because that was his job. It was his understanding of his role in the culture."[6]

I had crossed the boundary of what was normal regarding

status. Probably never before had this plant manager had a front-line employee approach him with such an outrageous request. I possessed very little cultural awareness at that time. I simply lived inside the environment, as did the supervisors who failed to notice my efforts and the plant manager who was perplexed by my initiative. What had changed was *my own idea* of what was possible. I had the eyes to see differently, yet I lacked the skills and development to make use of this new vision. I had no idea how to use communication as a strategy or how to consider objectives from management's point of view. I didn't understand how my own life history and background influenced the way I saw management or the way they saw me. Neither of us had the eyes to see the entire picture or the possibilities before us. We were in the dark, living out the cultural roles within which we operated.

Creating Versus Problem Solving

From my new vantage point, as one who spent over twenty years at the bottom, and almost the same number of years as a business owner, a leadership consultant, and coach, I can see how employees think and where companies are missing opportunities. I understand how to help bridge the gaps so that companies maximize employee engagement in the service of symbiotic value for value. The power to create is different from the power to solve problems. The power to create is about seeing differently—it's about challenging old beliefs and opening to new possibilities.

Creating a culture of employee engagement is not rocket science. Engagement is about the interest, initiative, and involvement that are born when employees' needs are met. Once the top leadership commits to understanding employee needs, the next step is to offer opportunities to meet those needs in alignment with the company's mission and goals. This requires aligning employees, interests and skills with business objectives. It's the ability to see employees, team members, associates—or whatever title you use—as more than cogs in a wheel, in order to engage their interests, initiatives, and involvement to help achieve business results.

Denise Bredfeldt remembers the days of being employed at SRC and eventually moving up in the company to play a significant role in the Great Game of Business program. "People were of equal value. There was never anyone you couldn't talk to because of their status in the organization. We drank beer together, we fished together, and we hunted together. It didn't make any difference where you were at on the totem pole," she said. [7]

During her employment at SRC, Bredfeldt went from working on the lines to running several SRC Subsidiaries, to documenting the methodology at The Great Game of Business to eventually running the Great Game herself. "It was a tremendous journey. Had a ball," she said.

Although Bredfeldt is now retired from the Great Game, she has been working on the Great Game Home Edition, a board game that teaches financial literacy. In addition, she is building a profitability game for teaching truck drivers how to make money. "I'm amazed at how many truck drivers sign a lease for $90,000 and haven't got a clue on how many miles they need to run to make their payment. It's scary, how ignorant America is when it comes to finances,"[8] she said.

From an entry-level production job and writing an underground newsletter to managing companies, teaching financial literacy, and building products that increase financial literacy across the country, Bredfeldt is an example of what is possible in the workplace if we have the eyes to see the opportunities and provide the right leadership and resources. The opportunities to engage employees are all around us yet are often missed because the signs are so subtle.

Missed Opportunities

I was in a department store at a mall making a purchase when I noticed a large bin of plastic clothes hangers. I asked the young clerk if they recycled the hangers. "No, we don't," she said. "We throw them away every day. It drives me crazy to see how wasteful this is to the environment."

"Have you made the suggestion to your boss about your ideas to recycle them?"

"Yes, I have, but she said that wasn't her job to figure that kind of stuff out."

Here is a young person who has an interest in the environment, who shows up and takes initiative to share an idea that would not only benefit the company but the environment, and her idea is shot down.

Let's look at the issues in this case: first is the culture. This anchor store at the mall has layers of bureaucracy, and the culture simply is not one of idea sharing from the bottom up. The second is leadership development and philosophy. Either the supervisor has not had leadership development that taught her how to engage with her people or she has not developed a personal leadership philosophy. The third issue is one of empowerment. Most likely, the supervisor does not even recognize her choice to take initiative; therefore, she simply ends the discussion with "That's not our job." Very likely, the fourth issue is a relationship issue: the supervisor may be too intimidated to go to her boss; therefore, she does not take initiative. Fifth, the leader has not been taught to see that idea sharing is a good sign that engagement could be increased. The flip side of idea sharing is complaining. Very often, when employees believe their ideas will be dismissed, they complain instead.

Complaining

From the drama perspective, it makes sense that leaders avoid or redirect complainers. From an enlightened perspective, however, leaders understand that complaining indicates someone is ready to take some initiative. There is one primary reason people complain: a desire or need is not being met. Within that framework, either the individual does not know what he wants and he complains as a way to express his frustration, or he does know what he wants but does not know how to meet the need. When people care about something, they are more likely to complain. How might this new understanding change our interpretation of the research that suggests disengaged employees contribute to dysfunctional workplace relationships?

During my factory years, I had one particular boss who was not necessarily the most enlightened leader. I recall setting a meeting with him because I was so frustrated about how hard we had worked only to feel defeated by mechanical problems. He said, "Hey, I didn't ask you to work here. If you don't like it, find another place to work."

After coaching thousands of frontline leaders in the years since, I have some hard-won insights to share. My boss most likely interpreted my frustration and desire for dialogue as complaining rather than engagement. When I went to my supervisor "complaining," all I really wanted was a pat on the back, someone to say, "I know you care a lot about your job and it must be frustrating to work so hard for nothing." I would have welcomed the suggestion to serve on a steering committee tasked with helping the mechanics fix the problem. In fact, I remember a particular time when I had an idea, but it was quashed because the supervisor was unwilling to listen. There is a lot to be learned from this experience, so I will share the story.

Due to new technology and high demand, the department merged two production lines to shoot product out of one line. This decision, which seemed so good on paper, produced a series of additional problems. There was a human being at the end of the line stacking the skid, pulling the skid, tagging the skid, wrapping the skid with a layer of cellophane, then hopping on the forklift to pull it away from the line before laying down another heavy oak skid to start over again.

Now, because two lines were merged, the product came barreling down the line at double the pace. This was no problem if the skid stacker was in shape and could keep up. However, there wasn't much leeway if the stacker fell behind. While the skid stacker was pulling the last load, the line continued to produce pallets of product at rapid speed as it rolled down the ramp, through a code dater to stamp the expiration date and other necessary information on the box, before the package would roll to the end of the very short line. Eventually, the product would back up and jam up inside the dater, which would then shut down the line.

One solution would have been to have two skid stackers; however, that defeated the productivity purpose. The second option would have been to lengthen the conveyer belt so that when boxes stacked up there was a little slack. I had planned to offer that idea when I was told I could always find another place to work.

Leaders Develop Other Leaders

Reading this, you might be thinking that I did not communicate strategically. You would be correct. That's like saying that a five-year-old should learn more effective ways to collaborate with his parents. The point is that employees do not know these skills. The truth is, neither do most leaders. People come to the workplace with the mind-sets they have grown up with. It is up to the company to develop leaders, and then it is up to the leaders to develop and teach employees.

Here is what I know after my decades of factory work: the ones who do the frontline work also have ideas to improve productivity, cut costs, and gain new customers. The best ideas do not come only from corporate headquarters, the marketing team, or the business unit managers. If frontline employees offer ideas that are not workable, it indicates that they do not understand the business, not that they are not capable. It also means that there are training opportunities available to help employees understand the business, so that in the future their ideas will be brilliant. If they complain, consider the complaining as a sign of interest, initiative, or involvement. This is an opportunity for the leader to develop another engaged leader. The idea sharing, listening, and respect helps to create a culture of collaboration.

Enlightened Engagement: Interest, Initiative, Involvement

From a drama perspective a leader may perceive that, employees are not engaged if they are negative, complaining, or refusing to volunteer for committees or overtime work. But enlightened leaders see complaining and negativity differently. Instead of quashing the complaints, enlightened leaders see an opportunity to develop the individual and an opportunity to practice using communication as a strategy.

From a more enlightened perspective, employees are already engaged; however, they are sometimes engaged in the wrong direction. They may be engaged in horseplay, writing underground newsletters, or complaining. Everything is energy, including our language, the thoughts we think, and the actions we take. Our energy is directed either in positive ways that align with the vision of the company or in negative, disruptive ways that put up barriers.

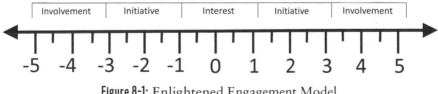

Figure 8-1: Enlightened Engagement Model

I have simplified engagement by offering what I call Enlightened Engagement, shown in Figure 8-1, using only three basic elements:

interest, initiative, and involvement. Using a number line, let's look at engagement from an enlightened perspective.

In the middle of the number line is interest. This is the neutral position. If someone is showing up for work, there is at least a baseline of interest. When someone is a model employee with regard to attendance, appearance, and work product, she has a higher level of interest in keeping the job. Now move to the right and see initiative. Initiative happens when an employee shares an idea or does something without being asked. Initiative is about using even more mind energy to do something that benefits the company. Then move another step to the right and see involvement. Now the employee has put some heart and soul into her initiative and is involved. This might show up as being a chair of a committee or asking to be mentored or volunteering to mentor someone else.

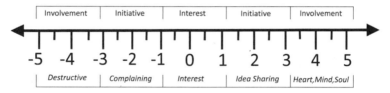

Figure 8-2: Enlightened Engagement Model

Now, looking at Figure 8-2, starting again at interest, but look to the left. You also see initiative, but look below the numbers on the number line to see how initiative on the negative side of neutral translates to complaining, while initiative on the right translates to idea sharing. Energy that moves to the left is negative initiative, which is usually some sort of complaining. Remember that a complaint is a signal that the person cares. This is where leadership opportunity and good coaching and communication skills come into play. A really good leader can take that complaint and shift it to the positive side of initiative.

Let's look again at initiative on the positive side. The young clerk who gave an idea to her supervisor about recycling plastic hangers took positive initiative. The supervisor shot down the idea with a "That's not our job" statement. Now the employee learns her ideas are of no use. If she feels frustrated, she goes to the negative side of initiative, and she complains about management to the customers or to her coworkers, who chime in and agree wholeheartedly.

As a leader you are either moving the energy forward into positive territory or allowing it to drift backward. When people do not have a vision or a purpose, when they are not excited and taking initiative, and when they are not involved, their engagement is flowing in the negative direction, which usually results in some type of drama.

What Leaders Can Do

When I was finishing my master's degree, my research pointed to two main observations: employees want to be respected and they want to be listened to. Simply taking the time to really listen to an idea or a problem makes employees feel respected rather than discounted.

Listening, taking action on employees' ideas, and then getting back to them about how their ideas were used contributes to good workplace relationships. These approaches dramatically increase the likelihood of employee engagement.

As Lauren Dixon, CEO of Dixon Schwabl, said, "If somebody comes to me with a great idea I don't sit on it, I take action. My promise back to my team members has always been, if you come to me with a great idea I will get back to you within forty-eight hours with a yes, or a how about if we twist it and turn it this way kind of answer. I don't take their ideas and input lightly."[9]

Remember Harold, the meat manager whom upper leadership did not invite to the trade show? Harold wanted to be involved. Even if the executives could not justify sending him to the trade show in Vegas, they could have sought his opinion and involved

Harold in the plans to change the meat display. The interest, initiative, and involvement number line runs both ways. Engagement is a symbiotic exchange of value that reinforces relationships. When leaders ignore this fact, they don't hamper engagement, they simply shift it to the negative direction.

No matter how much Harold might have enjoyed his job, he now has little motivation to collaborate with the decision makers to ensure success because they do not consider the role he plays in their success. In fact, his motivation is just the opposite—to prove that the changes were not well thought out. His commitment to do his job well is tested each time a customer searches for the turkey cutlets that have been moved from their former case. Harold has a choice to step up and help or to stand by and prove his point: Upper management should have asked his opinion before making changes. His own character will determine the choice he makes. This is not a story about Harold or a judgment on what choice he may or may not make. Harold's story is an example of what happens in companies every day and a reminder about human nature. We all want to be right. Involving or consulting with employees on decisions that affect them provides a structure that virtually eliminates the "us versus them" mentality and provides the power to create engagement inside the corporation.

Executive Summary

- ➤ Companies need to define engagement, just as they define leadership.
- ➤ Engagement is a symbiotic exchange of value for value.
- ➤ When people grow, they require different types of engagement.
- ➤ Enlightened engagement is interest, initiative, and involvement.

Wisdom Exercises

1. When an employee complains, what can you do to shift the energy to positive initiative?
2. Make a list of the ways you see negative engagement in your company.
3. Name two ways you can start showing interest in your employees.

CHAPTER 9

Empowerment

Power is contingent upon the proper use of power already in possession.

—Charles Haanel

Andrew, the manager of housekeeping at the rehabilitation center, had just told his staff member Janet that she could find another job if she didn't change her attitude. Andrew's stress comes from trying to manage employees who just don't seem to care. Why can't they just do their jobs?

Janet resents Andrew's harsh leadership style and only tolerates her job, showing up for the paycheck. She has never considered that there might be opportunities for advancement inside the company. She doesn't ask questions. She wasn't hired to think, because she's at the bottom of the totem pole. Janet does not feel a sense of pride in her workplace, her profession, or herself, nor does she feel empowered. She doesn't even know what the word means.

Julie also works in housekeeping but is excited about the options to advance her career and knows she has the enthusiasm and talent to do so. She uses good judgment to make sure her guests are taken care of, and she takes pride in her job.

While they both work in housekeeping positions, Janet and

Julie have two vastly different experiences, due largely to the company they work for. Julie works for the Ritz-Carlton Hotel Company and Janet works for—well, I'll let you fill in the blank. Two of the service values of Ritz-Carlton are: "I have the opportunity to continuously learn and grow, and I am empowered to create unique, memorable, and personal experiences for our guests." If a guest is unhappy, Julie takes responsibility and makes the choices to make things right. The Ritz-Carlton has trained her well, and Julie does not see herself as "just a housekeeper" but as a lady, serving other ladies and gentlemen. She is proud of her workplace, her profession, and herself.

Companies that consciously create empowered cultures do more than gain profits and reduce turnover. These companies actually shift the identities of their employees. The key to understanding empowerment is to first understand the nature of power.

Power Versus Powerlessness

Every behavior is an expression of the perception of power or lack thereof (see Figure 9-1); I refer to this as the E-2 Model (Express Experience). When Andrew screams at his staff of housekeepers, it is because he feels powerless and is trying to ramp up his power by using force. Our behavior and language express what we are experiencing. A heavy sigh expresses the frustration we feel. A laugh following the frustration expresses relief. Janet disengages from her job because she experiences powerlessness, while Julie actively engages because she experiences a sense of power.

These experiences and expressions happen so automatically that we don't give much thought to them, nor do we think much about how our outward behaviors and language express inner emotions. It doesn't matter whether your experience of a situation is based on fact or not. If you perceive something to be so, then for you it is so. Thus, outward expression always mirrors the experience.

Empowerment

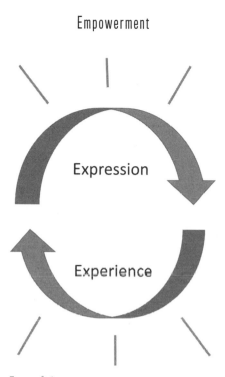

Figure 9-1: Express Experience Model

When we don't get what we want and don't know how to get what we want, we experience powerlessness. When people work for a paycheck, with no other purpose, they experience powerlessness. When employees seek recognition for a job well done but instead are asked to do more with less, the experience of "never enough" turns quickly into burnout and disengagement.

How an employee perceives these experiences is influenced by her personal history. It shapes her thoughts, feelings, and, ultimately, the story she makes up about what happened, how things work, and how things are. In chapter 5, on change, we talked about the four quadrants, with quadrant three and four identified as change that was unwanted. Any change that is experienced as unwanted creates in an individual the experience of powerlessness.

Powerlessness always expresses as drama, ranging from violence, aggressiveness, manipulation, and complaints to a victim mentality and a feeling of hopelessness. For example, when a front line employee complains, it is because on some level he wants something but doesn't know how to get it. Thus, he expresses his experience of powerlessness by complaining or giving up.

When the manager perceives the complaining as disruptive to his desired result, he uses force to try to regain control. His response (expression) is to create a new policy or fire someone without warning. Or he puts someone on a job he hates to teach him a lesson. The manager tells the employee, "I didn't ask you to work here. Find yourself another job," thus resorting to manipulation and force to end the controversy rather than using power to create something new. Force is simply another expression of powerlessness, just as stealing is an expression of a poverty mentality instead of an expression of an abundance mentality. Confidence mirrors power and low self-esteem mirrors powerlessness. Every experience manifests into language or behavior that mirrors the experience.

When we do not understand how power works and do not understand the impact of powerlessness on our personal and organizational lives, we contribute more drama to the very problems we are trying to eliminate. For example, the hard-driving employee, like Andrew, who is promoted to supervisor without the proper leadership development will eventually experience powerlessness. Because they don't have the tools or the wisdom they need to do their jobs well, these underdeveloped leaders experience frustration and are prone to expressing behaviors that inhibit teamwork. The end result is absenteeism, lost productivity, or turnover, which affect the company's profitability.

Most leaders do not recognize the root cause of the dysfunction. They ignore the cause, and instead of looking at the leadership, they put together an engagement initiative. This is precisely why we need enlightened leaders who have the wisdom and discernment to be role models for the effective use of power, and to promote empowerment through balanced choice and responsibility.

Balance

In every empowered workplace, you will see balance. One value balances another, as do opportunity and risk and choice and responsibility. In my work, I have come to realize that many hard-driving executives or owners do not necessarily believe in balance. They believe only in profits, not in people. They believe in strategy but not culture. They believe in productivity but not passion.

The either-or way of thinking indicates a major misunderstanding of universal laws. It does not matter if you believe in balance or not, just as it does not matter if you believe in gravity. It does not matter that you do not believe in a regular break or see the connection between rejuvenation and productivity. You can work around the clock and demand higher productivity, but eventually the body wears out and requires rest. Overwork without adequate rest results in stress hormones flowing through your body that express as temper and aggression. Not listening to the body's need for balance produces relationship drama at home and at work, which leads to more signs that you need to balance work with rest. When the signs are totally ignored, balance will be attained through a stroke or heart attack, ensuring that the body receives rest. Just as work and rest must be balanced, the profits and people equation must be balanced. Promoting hard-driving managers who have no leadership skills and no opportunities for development leads to absenteeism, then turnover, both signs that the profits and people equation needs attention.

Companies want employees to do more than show up, and employees want stimulating work, development opportunities, and creative ways to share their talents. When the company provides these opportunities for employees, the employees provide added value for the company. In short, balance will be restored eventually. The question is whether it is by choice or by circumstances.

Balancing Choice and Responsibility

The principle of balancing choice with responsibility works in every industry, company, and government agency, as well as in personal life. The more choices you have, the more responsibility is required.

Every corporate scandal that results in an executive going to prison is a snapshot of what happens when the choices made outweigh the responsibility accepted. In contrast, every successful turnaround of a struggling company is an example of leaders and employees successfully balancing choice with responsibility.

One of my favorite examples of a leader who balances choice and responsibility is the CEO of Barry-Wehmiller, Bob Chapman, whom I told you about in chapter 7. At just thirty years of age and fueled by the intensity of his father's passing, Chapman was ready to put his MBA education and business knowledge, as well as his accounting and CPA degree, to good use. Chapman perceived that Barry-Wehmiller was in an old industry, and he knew he had to find new markets in order to grow the company. Through acquisitions, Barry-Wehmiller's revenue grew dramatically from $18 million to $72 million over the course of four years, making the company and Chapman's leadership the talk of St. Louis.

"I had lived so long in a company that never grew, was never exciting, that just existed, so that when we started growing from $18 million to $72 million I was recruiting people all over the world to work for our company,"[1] Chapman says in his *Defining Moments* video on YouTube. Then, in 1982, everything started going south—as a result of the debt the company had taken on, the bank pulled its loan. Barry-Wehmiller operated without credit for almost a year. Not knowing whether he would be able to meet payroll was a defining moment for Chapman. He realized he had not implemented the financial discipline he'd been taught. Through unwanted change and *imbalance,* Chapman learned many lessons about business relationships, financial discipline, and balance.

"Never tell me, 'I have a good relationship with my banker.' When you move out of risk profile with your banker, it's over if you put your business to risk. The foundation upon which you can build a company is financial discipline and balance,"[2] Chapman said in the same video, noting that his company was the bank's biggest client at the time the loan was pulled. Growth that is not balanced with discipline leads to unnecessary problems. The Barry-Wehmiller story illustrates that, when it comes to power, even solid relationships dissolve when your business decisions threaten your partner's interests, thus decreasing the value-for-value balance.

Today, through the fiscal and leadership lessons Chapman has learned, Barry-Wehmiller has transformed into a company that focuses on "truly human leadership," where the real bottom line is the way people are treated: employee growth is supported and success is measured by the way the company touches people's lives. An outgrowth of the new philosophies has led to Barry-Wehmiller University (BWU) offering classes to participants across the country to teach them about truly human leadership.

Most of us in the workplace are not CEOs, nor do we have to wrestle with the magnitude of choice and responsibility that belongs to global business owners or high-level executives, yet we can get great insights—from both organizational and leadership perspectives—from these top leaders. Through reading about their experiences, we can look at how the themes of balance, choice, and responsibility run through the company's structure, and how to apply these universal lessons to leadership to improve our own organizations. Next, we will look at three very different organizations—Morning Star, the City of Rancho Cordova in California, and The Great Game of Business—to see examples of empowerment in the workplace.

Empowerment at Morning Star

I had the opportunity to interview Paul Green, a former employee with the Morning Star Company, the world's leading tomato processor. During his years of employment Green wore many hats, as almost everyone does at Morning Star. His interest in self-management led him to co-founding Morning Star's Self-Management Institute in 2008. The Self-Management Institute is the research and education organization focusing on the development of superior systems and principles for organizing people. Its mission is to instill these principles in the minds of the company's clients and colleagues.

At Morning Star, employees experience power by *opting in* rather than being forced to do potentially unfulfilling work that does not ignite their passions. Green said:

> There is a tendency in business to think about people being cells on a spreadsheet. There's a perspective out there when we need someone to do a job that all we have to do is define the job, list the activities and skills required, then try to find someone that matches. The truth is, no one will match the job perfectly. People are not cells on a spreadsheet. We recognize that people bring interests and passions to the workplace, and we allow them to form an odd-shaped job around those interests and passions. People will enact those passions and interests. People can find their optimum potential and performance if they have choice and we let them opt in."[3]

With all the choices available, how does Morning Star balance the power of choice with responsibility? Through "stepping stones" (progress reports), relationships, and transparency. Green noted:

Our stepping stones are public domain. Anyone can go look at anyone's stepping stones. They create social or peer pressure to perform. We have a more formal version at the business unit level. Every business unit gets together to evaluate past performance and go through a semiformal planning process and they present to their colleagues. Their peers matter a lot. The mechanisms we have in place are social. People think more like entrepreneurs, and the thrill is to use intellectual capital and relationships to get business results.

Morning Star is a great example of what is possible even in industries like manufacturing where it's difficult to imagine front-line workers having the ability to impact high-level decisions like hiring, firing, purchasing machinery, and designing their own job.

Empowerment at the City of Rancho Cordova

Most of us think of government as a bureaucracy that tends toward wasteful spending and systems that contribute to dependency and dysfunction rather than empowerment. The City of Rancho Cordova, California, is consciously changing that perception. Stacey Peterson, the chief people officer whom I introduced earlier, and Joe Chinn, the assistant city manager, had a lot to say about creating structures in government that promote empowerment. Peterson said:

A lot of times citizens can see government as "Well, here is my problem, so fix it." We have instead said, "No, we're here to facilitate a solution to that." We have employed the entrepreneurial spirit. Our mission is to be catalysts, facilitators, brokers, and educators in helping our community solve problems through partnerships. We promote empowerment for all of our employees but also for the purpose of empowering the community."[4]

Chinn added, "We are not here to create an empire. Some governments seem to get bigger and bigger and bigger. We're a contract city. We get funding out to the right agencies that can solve the problems better and more cost effectively."[5]

The goal is to lead others by providing resources and knowledge to empower citizens to easily find their own solutions. Through the power of knowledge and partnerships, citizens become empowered rather than dependent.

Empowerment at the Great Game of Business

The Great Game of Business is not only a book, The Great Game of Business is the educational wing of SRC, and is now the largest and best-known resource for open-book management training and education, with more than six thousand companies trained worldwide. As you might remember from chapter 6, The Great Game evolved after Jack Stack found investors and secured a loan to purchase SRC from Harvester. Stack began opening the books with employees, teaching them the financials and sharing in the rewards. This led to a gigantic turnaround, which led to an article in *Inc.* magazine, which prompted other business owners to become interested Stack's methods.

Rich Armstrong, president of The Great Game, said, "The cornerstone of The Great Game of Business is knowledge. Our goal is to make sure every employee in the organization has a comprehensive understanding of business, from how the business operates financially, and how the business operates in the market place."[6]

In his book *Concept of the Corporation,*[7] management consultant Peter Drucker said that foremen should be trained in every discipline of the company because they can't understand the business unless they've seen every part of it. That's been Armstrong's philosophy in teaching all employees about business:

> When employees understand your business, it doesn't matter what discipline they're in or what role they're playing in the company. You would make a better decision for the company based on that comprehensive understanding. Unfortunately, we train and we educate a role, responsibility, or discipline. Accountants know everything about accounting but they don't know what sales and marketing's about. Guess what? When an accountant makes a decision, they're making it in the best interest of accounting, not in the best interest of the company.[8]

Every year, The Great Game of Business announces its All-Star Awards to the companies practicing open-book management. Armstrong said that every year he hears from clients, "The reason I got involved with The Great Game of Business was for my financial or business literacy. What actually happened was renewed interest from my employees and more connection with the business."[9] What starts as an intention to teach financial literacy becomes transformational because employees start thinking like owners.

Elements of Empowerment

Whatever the industry or business model, you will find a combination of these six elements of empowerment: clarity, purpose, people, knowledge, resources, and resourcefulness. Your company's mission tells you *why* you do what you do. From the perspective of creating, clarity is about the *what*. Aligning *what* and *why* is key to success.

The Ritz-Carlton is an example of clearly defining the "what," or the desired result, in daily operations that are aligned with its credo:

The Ritz-Carlton Hotel is a place where the genuine care and comfort of our guests is our highest mission. We pledge to provide the finest personal service and facilities for our guests, who will always enjoy a warm, relaxed, yet refined ambience. The Ritz-Carlton experience enlivens the senses, instills well-being, and fulfills even the unexpressed wishes and needs of our guests.[10]

Employees are oriented on day one, and then thoroughly trained and given the resources to accomplish the company's vision. So, the first step in empowerment is knowing the "what" on a day-to-day basis.

The second element is about the "who," the employees. Managers often fail in considering the people. They know the "what," but then they get stuck on the rock called "how." It is the employees who will fulfill the mission of the organization, and get the company to the desired end result. If you want to create a new culture of empowerment, you should not work hours and hours trying to figure out the how. You first must get clear on the "what" and then seek out other people who have already accomplished what you want to achieve. Before acting, you need to consider the talent you already have inside your company and seek their opinion. Taking action without first seeking information from your other stakeholders is a waste of resources.

The Morning Star Company offers a great example of a model that relies on tapping into the talents of the company's own people. It is the people on the floor who make the decisions. Any employee who needs a new piece of equipment has the power to purchase the equipment, as long as she talks to the other stakeholders, does the necessary research, and gets agreement that the decision is best for the company. As an employee of Morning Star, you seek out the relationships you need to cultivate support, and you report your success to other people, who become your accountability partners.

My friends Christine and Joe Daues, founders of Granolove, a food manufacturer of healthy gluten-free granola, exemplify the third element of empowerment: purpose. The idea for Granolove started in Christine's kitchen, out of a desire to provide a healthy breakfast alternative for her family. With the challenges of starting a company, Christine and Joe faced their own dark night of the soul when they found out that their unborn child would have physical abnormalities. "They told me that she has only three fingers on her left hand. She's missing a bone in her left arm. She will have a shorter leg,"[11] Christine said.

Then something changed. Joe and Christine decided to find purpose in their circumstances. Joe said, "After a period of mourning, we bucked up and said, we are going to plow forward. We will make something positive out of this. They tell us they can't regrow bones in children—we are going to do something to make that happen."[12]

As a result of their challenges, Christine and Joe have a renewed sense of purpose to make Granolove profitable. Christine said:

> We hold a vision, that one day she will have bones that can be grown. It is not out of the realm of possibility. We follow this research. Soldiers are coming back with legs blown off and are regenerating bone and nerve tissue. When Jude is twenty-five years old there may be a possibility for her and we want to be a part of making that happen. We have great aspirations for this company to make it grow so that our profits are helping sustain us but also doing something for medical research. In that regard, spiritually I live and die by that focus.[13]

Today, Christine and Joe give 10 percent of their profits to Shriners Hospitals for Children, an organization at the forefront of pediatric orthopedics, as they purposefully grow their company to fulfill a greater good.

The fourth element of empowered cultures is knowledge. Besides knowledge gained from experience, the most valuable knowledge comes from other people who have already succeeded in reaching a similar goal. Knowledge from other people shaves thousands of hours off your learning curve. I have found that many high-level leaders have a difficult time asking for advice or learning from others. This is a major mistake. In short, a learning mind-set helps you get to your result faster. More formal ways of obtaining knowledge come through executive education, leadership development, mentoring, coaching, or consulting. The Great Game of Business is a prime example of a company committed to sharing knowledge inside the company and, through formal educational offerings, helping other companies create empowered cultures using open-book management.

The fifth element of empowerment is resources, and the sixth is resourcefulness. Without the resources to get the job done, employees cannot act from power. Instead, they will be frustrated. The problem most managers have is, "There's no room in the budget." Providing resources is different from teaching resourcefulness. When budget is a barrier, teaching resourcefulness is more empowering than saying a flat-out "No." When resources are not readily available, it is easy to get stuck in old ideas of what is *not* possible, blaming the budget and complaining about the way things are. Empowerment is about the ability to act—the ability to create, even when resources seem to be inadequate. Often, the resources come through resourcefulness.

The City of Rancho Cordova demonstrates how providing resources through knowledge and teaching resourcefulness in the community. For example, when citizens need help, instead of fixing the problem, Rancho Cordova provides information about resources so that informed citizens can become resourceful and make the choices they need, rather than looking to government to fix the problem.

Signs of Empowerment

Using the Express Experience model I discussed earlier in the chapter, it's relatively easy to see which is being expressed, power or powerlessness. The signs of empowerment include:

- People asking for what they want
- Sharing of ideas
- Clarity of intention
- Purpose
- Teamwork
- Responsible language
- Initiative
- Pride in one's work

By contrast, negativity, complaints, and blaming indicate a lack of empowerment, which almost always results in lower levels of engagement. Almost every time workplace drama erupts, employees get the blame. Over and over, I have heard stories about disengaged employees or a queen bee who cannot be "managed." This tells me that the leadership is not empowered and that it does not model empowerment in the workplace.

When I see supervisors and managers complain, fail to ask for what they want, and exhibit negativity, I know that these leaders are unaware of their own expression of powerlessness. The problem here is one of awareness and lack of personal responsibility. I have yet to meet a leader at any level who thinks he is part of the problem. Let me share a story.

I was doing a leadership retreat for a group of administrators. One of the administrators, Becky, admitted she felt overwhelmed and burned out. She had too much work, too few resources, and she didn't trust her employees enough to delegate some of her workload. In a nutshell, Becky felt powerless. Needless to say, her experience expressed as frustration.

Becky could certainly see that her employees had a negative mind-set, didn't know how to ask for what they wanted, and often waited for her to fix their problems. But she didn't see that she had the very same problem. Becky could not seem to grasp the idea that she had choices, and all she had to do was see the choices and implement them.

It was after the seminar's lunch break that Becky experienced her first aha moment; I went to the front of the room to bring everyone back to attention, and I noticed the projector was out of focus, so I adjusted it. After the screen came into focus, I heard Becky let out a loud sigh and loudly profess, "Thank goodness! That had been driving me crazy for the last two hours!" After the laughter died down, I asked, "What choices did you have?"

"Well—I was too afraid to ask you to fix it."

"That's not the question. The question is, what choices did you have? You have been miserable for two hours. What choices did you have?"

"I hinted to her to fix it." [Pointing to a coworker in jest]

"So you did ask someone to fix it but she said no?"

"Yes, she said no."

"What other choice did you have?"

"I could have asked you to fix it."

"Yes, or you could have come up during lunch and fixed it yourself."

"I was afraid I would look stupid."

"So you were more worried about looking stupid, and therefore you were willing to be miserable and put your focus on the out-of-focus projector rather than ask for what you want?"

"Did you make the projector out of focus on purpose?" asked one of the participants who was watching this scenario play out. I had to laugh. I couldn't have produced this kind of response if I had tried to orchestrate it. The gift to the participants was a living example of how easily we see dysfunction in others while being blind to our own.

The same blind spots happen on the executive level when well-meaning leaders decide to change the culture by increasing engagement or teaching employees to become empowered, while at the same time expressing powerlessness themselves. I have personally witnessed employees giving ideas to their boss and getting a response of, "That's not possible," or "That can't be done," rather than hearing from the boss, "What is possible?" or "What ideas do you have?"

All the engagement initiatives and employee training in the world will not create the changes needed if the leaders themselves express symptoms of powerlessness. In fact, instead of working to change culture, look at what is being *expressed,* and then work to create a new experience, starting with your own development and the development of other leaders. Then your culture will start to shift. Engagement and empowerment are results not initiatives.

Empowered Leaders

Many might say that empowerment starts at the top, but empowerment starts within. As a leader—one who is in a role of authority—there are many things you can delegate, but there is one thing that belongs only to you: your own personal and leadership development. Blame is never a good investment, but developing yourself is. You will be out of alignment with any set of values if you point a finger at your disempowered employees but you yourself never see any choices or express any signs of powerful thinking.

It is out of alignment, too, to criticize a company that does not have a budget for development if you aren't willing to invest a few dollars on a book, CD, or retreat that could elevate your skills and change your life.

I often tell frontline leaders and employees who are discouraged about the lack of company budget for development that if they commit to their own development over the course of a few years, they can get a job anywhere and then become aligned with a company that has the same values around development that they do.

No doubt, the best formula for leadership development includes both the company and the individual's commitment to leadership growth. When the company invests in leadership development and the person being developed is willing to learn, grow, and develop her own definition of leadership—that's *magic!* This is a joint commitment. The company commits to investing and provides the resources, and the individual commits to living by her stated values in alignment with, and in service to, the overall mission of the company.

Companies tend to attract employees who embody the demonstrated values of their cultures. When the workplace has a boss who complains and does not model empowerment, it's unlikely many employees will exhibit creativity, initiative, or high levels of performance.

Because empowerment starts on the inside, even those who do not hold a leadership position have access to personal power, which is available even in the worst of workplace climates. There are always choices; however, our lack of awareness can keep us imprisoned. We are often like Dorothy in *The Wizard of Oz*. We have the power but don't recognize it. Our power is not in a pair of ruby slippers, which are easy to see, but in the choices always available, but which are sometimes invisible to us. The first step is to recognize that the power exists. My own journey is about waking up to the fact that the choices are there, whether you recognize them or not. When I worked at the factory, there were always choices to continue my education, and there were choices available for me to grow personally. The problem was that I didn't *see* the choices for a long time. It was the drama of dissatisfaction that eventually became a stepping-stone onto the bridge of enlightenment. With a new vision, a decision to take responsibility, and an awakening to my choices, I changed my life dramatically.

No matter what your level in your organization—C-suite executive, manager, supervisor, or frontline employee—the chief lesson for you is the same one Dorothy learned in *The Wizard of Oz*: We keep looking to the man behind the curtain for the answers, only to find we had the power all along.

Executive Summary

➢ Every behavior is an expression of power or powerlessness.
➢ When you see your choices you become empowered.
➢ Choice and responsibility must be balanced.
➢ Clarity, purpose, people, knowledge, resources, and resourcefulness are elements of empowerment.

Wisdom Exercises

1. Describe the signs that indicate empowerment in your workplace.
2. Discuss how leaders can promote empowerment in the workplace.
3. Complete the sentence: one way I contribute to a current workplace problem is...

Conclusion: From Drama to Enlightenment

If you can't resolve your problems in peace, you can't solve them with war.

—Somalian proverb

There are no perfect leaders. A leader who is enlightened in one particular area, may struggle in another. When you find yourself tempted to judge harshly, or when tempted to put someone on a pedestal, try to remember that we are all in this together. It is very difficult to learn from anyone when you see them as inferior or superior.

We are at different points on the journey, playing our own game, learning our own lessons. The real challenge of enlightened leadership is to do your own inner work so that you become a light in the dark. There is plenty of work to be done for every single one of us, no matter what our position, education, or status.

Today's leader needs more than position, power, or business acumen. Today's leader needs more than self-management, communication skills, or emotional intelligence. The world needs leaders who are aligned, aware, and accountable, leaders who have the eyes to see what is possible and who have the power to create the right environment, empowerment, and engagement. We need enlightened leaders who balance choice and power with wisdom and responsibility, leaders who embrace both inner leadership growth and strong business results, and who model the mind-sets and actions that can transform the cultures they lead.

If leaders do not balance choice with responsibility, how can they prevent entitlement? If they do not have the eyes of discernment, how can they create a new vision? If they do not own the mastery of self, how can they model excellence? If they do not recognize the choices, how can they promote empowerment? If leaders are not aligned, how can they be enlightened?

Yet we live in a world of paradox, contrast, and contradiction.

With enlightenment comes growth.

With growth comes instability.

With instability comes uncertainty.

With uncertainty comes drama.

With drama comes the opportunity for enlightenment.

There is no day without night, no right without left, no good without evil, no yin without yang, no challenge without opportunity, and no enlightenment without drama. So then how does one become a No-Drama Leader?[

The paradox is this: To become a no-drama leader, a leader must use drama as a transformative agent to reveal the power of conscious choice. It is then that drama can be viewed not as an obstacle, but as a stepping stone onto a bridge of enlightenment. The power is always in the choices we make every day.

Every day we can bet on profits or on people.

Every day we get the chance to show judgment or show compassion.

Every day we have an opportunity to act as a teacher or as a student.

Every day we can see ourselves and others as broken or whole.

Every day we can define success as what we have and what we do, or we can define success by who we are.

Every day we can become part of the problem or part of the solution.

We stand at the point of choice.

We can choose to continue on the *either-or* path, or we can choose the road to *both-and*.

We can make great profits while cultivating great people. We can exhibit good judgment while showing great compassion. We can see ourselves as both teacher and student. We can see that we are all the same—sometimes broken, but always whole.

We can choose to define success not only by what we have and what we do, but by who we are.

We can criticize the powers that be or we can become the power that is.

Moving from drama to enlightenment takes courage: one act of courage at a time.

NOTES

Introduction

1. Heather Joyner, phone conversation with author, January 2012.
2. Marlene Chism, *Stop Workplace Drama: Train Your Team to Have No Complaints, No Excuses, and No Regrets* (John Wiley and Sons, 2011).
3. "No. 1 Reason People Quit Their Jobs," Netscape, August 14, 2014, Jobshttp://webcenters.netscape.compuserve.com/whatsnew/package .jsp?name=fte/quitjobs/quitjobs.
4. *Human Capital Trends Report for 2014,* Deloitte Consulting LLP and Bersin by Deloitte, January 17, 2014, http://www.deloitte.com/assets/ Dcom-Namibia/GlobalHumanCapitalTrends2014_030714.pdf.
5. *Human Capital Trends Report for 2014,* Deloitte Consulting LLP and Bersin by Deloitte, January 17, 2014, http://www.deloitte.com/assets/ Dcom-Namibia/GlobalHumanCapitalTrends2014_030714.pdf, 7.
6. Simon Sinek, *Why Leaders Eat Last,* YouTube video, 12:40, posted by 99U, December 4, 2013, https://www.youtube.com/watch?v=ReRc HdeUG9Y.
7. Peter F. Drucker, "Managing Knowledge Means Managing Oneself," *Leader to Leader* 16 (Spring 2000), http://rlaexp.com/studio/biz/ conceptual_resources/authors/peter_drucker/mkmmo_org.pdf.

Chapter 1

1. Bob Funk, interview by author, audio recording, August 7, 2014.
2. Bob Funk, interview by author, audio recording, August 7, 2014.
3. *Merriam-Webster Dictionary Online,* "alignment," August 14, 2014, http://www.merriam-webster.com/dictionary/alignment.
4. Frances Hesselbein, interview by author, audio recording, August 20, 2014.
5. "Domestic Violence in Detail," *USA Today,* October 2, 2014.

6. Brent Schrotenboer, "Richie Incognito's Bully Reputation Goes Back to 2002," *USA Today,* November 5, 2013, http://www.usatoday.com/story/sports/nfl/2013/11/05/incognito-bully-accusations-nebraska-reshman/3439819/.

7. Deborah Rozman, "Heart Mastery," July 11, 2014, http://heartmastery.com/files/Deborah%20Rozman%20Bio.pdf.

8. Emily Esfahani Smith, "Social Connection Makes a Better Brain," the *Atlantic,* online edition, October 29, 2013, http://www.theatlantic.com/health/archive/2013/10/social-connection-makes-a-better-brain/280934/.

9. Megan Griffo, "Doctor Walks 6 Miles Through Snow Storm to Perform Emergency Brain Surgery," *The Huffington Post,* January 31, 2014, http://www.huffingtonpost.com/2014/01/30/dr-zenko-hrynkiw-6-miles-brain-surgery_n_4697195.html.

10. Eckhart Tolle, *The New Earth and Practicing the Power of Now: A Guide to Spiritual Enlightenment,* (Novato, CA: New World Library, 2004).

11. Peter Senge, *The Fifth Discipline: The Art and Practice of the Learning Organization,* (New York: Crown Publishing Group, 2006), 312.

12. Press Association, "Sir Bradley Wiggins Says Children Were Bullied Over Armstrong Drug Scandal," *The Guardian,* February 5, 2014, http://www.theguardian.com/sport/2014/feb/05/bradley-wiggings-lance-armstrong-children.

13. "Colo. Principal Says She Was Fired Over 'Disrespectful' Policy Towards Poor Children," CBSnews.com, January 8, 2014, http://www.cbsnews.com/news/former-colo-principal-claims-fired-for-fighting-student-humiliation/.

Chapter 2

1. Daniel Goleman, *Focus: The Hidden Driver of Excellence* (New York: Harper, 2013), 69.

2. James 2:18 (New American Standard Bible).

3. Dr. Kevin Fleming, interview by author, audio recording, March 3, 2008.

4. Dr. David Simon, interview by author, audio recording, December 12, 2010.

5. Dr. David Simon, interview by author, audio recording, December 12, 2010.

6. E-mail to author from private client, March 11, 2009.
7. Tim Boden, e-mail to author, October 22, 2014.

Chapter 3

1. Interview with private client, March 12, 2010.
2. Interview with private client, June 16, 2010.
3. Stacey Peterson, interview by author, audio recording, August 13, 2014.
4. *Wikipedia,* "List of Corporate Collapses and Scandals," September 5, 2014, http://en.wikipedia.org/wiki/List_of_corporate_collapses_and _scandals.
5. The Free Dictionary, http://www.thefreedictionary.com/.
6. John Reynolds, interview by author, audio recording, August 15, 2014.
7. John Reynolds, interview by author, audio recording, August 15, 2014
8. John Reynolds, interview by author, audio recording, August 15, 2014.
9. Lauren Dixon, interview by author, audio recording, July 22, 2014.
10. Lauren Dixon, interview by author, audio recording, July 22, 2014.
11. Lauren Dixon, interview by author, audio recording, July 22, 2014.
12. Carol S. Dweck, *Mindset: The New Psychology of Success* (New York: Ballantine Books, 2007), 15.
13. Lauren Dixon, interview by author, audio recording, July 22, 2014.
14. Lauren Dixon, interview by author, audio recording, July 22, 2014.
15. Lauren Dixon, interview by author, audio recording, July 22, 2014.

Part 2 Introduction

1. Dr. Kevin Fleming, interview by author, audio recording, February 4, 2010.

Chapter 4

1. Author interview with public safety professional, September 24, 2014.
2. Bob Funk, interview by author, audio recording, August 7, 2014.
3. *Top Five Threats Facing Business Today,* Express Employment Professionals. July 1, 2014; Express Employment Professionals, Oklahoma City, OK.
4. Bob Funk, interview by author, audio recording, August 7, 2014.
5. Stephen Covey, *The One Thing That Changes Everything* (New York: Free Press, 2008).
6. Dr. David Simon, interview by author, audio recording, March 4, 2010.
7. Elaine Brink, interview by author, audio recording, August 5, 2014.

8. Kashmir Hill, "OfficeMax Blames Data Broker for 'Daughter Killed in Car Crash' Letter," Forbes.com. http://www.forbes.com/sites/kashmirhill /2014/01/22/officemax-blames-data-broker-for-daughter -killed-in-car-crash-letter/.

9. Adam Kissel, "East Stroudsburg University Suspends Innocent Professor for Weeks over Facebook Comments," Foundation for Individual Rights in Education (FIRE), April 5, 2010, http://www.thefire.org/east -stroudsburg-university-suspends-innocent-professor-for-weeks-over -facebook-comments/.

10. Marshall Goldsmith, "Try Feedforward Instead of Feedback," adapted from *Leader to Leader,* Summer 2002, http://www.marshallgoldsmithlibrary .com/cim/articles_display.php?aid=110.

Chapter 5

1. Denise Bredfeldt, interview by author, audio recording, September 18, 2014.

2. Denise Bredfeldt, interview by author, audio recording, September 18, 2014.

3. Christopher Vaughan, "Interview with Jack Stack," The Center for Ethics and Entrepreneurship, April 11, 2011, http://www.ethicsandentre preneurship.org/20110411/interview-with-jack-stack/.

4. Marlene Chism, *Stop Workplace Drama: Train Your Team to Have No Excuses, No Complaints and No Regrets* (New Jersey: John Wiley & Sons, 2011), 49–55.

5. David Rock, *Your Brain at Work: Strategies for Overcoming Distraction, Regaining Focus, and Working Smarter All Day Long* (New York: Harper Business), 227.

6. Edgar Schein, interview by author, audio recording, August 15, 2014.

7. Edgar Schein, interview by author, audio recording, August 15, 2014.

8. Edgar Schein, interview by author, audio recording, August 15, 2014.

Chapter 6

1. Jia Lynn Yang and Amrita Jayakumar, "Target Says Up to 70 Million More Customers Were Hit by December Data Breach, *Washington Post,* January 10, 2014, http://www.washingtonpost.com/business/ economy/target-says-70-million-customers-were-hit-by-dec -data-breach-more-than-first-reported/2014/01/10/0ada1026-79fe -11e3-8963-b4b654bcc9b2_story.html.

2. Larry Baum, interview by author, audio recording, August 12, 2014.

3. "Fletcher Allen's Ex-CEO Admits to Fraud," *The Barre Montpelier Times Argus,* January 19, 2005, http://timesargus.com/apps/pbcs.dll/article?AID=/20050119/NEWS/501190337/1002.

4. Roberta Nubile, "Fletcher Allen's CEO Melinda Estes: No Soloist," *Vermont Woman,* April 2009, http://www.vermontwoman.com/articles/2009/0409/estes.html.

5. Melinda Estes, MD, *Healthy Food in Health Care,* YouTube video, 6:20, posted by Fletcher Allen, December 2, 2010, https://www.youtube.com/watch?v=yHYejTZh_0I.

6. Melinda Estes, MD, *Healthy Food in Health Care,* YouTube video, 0:37, posted by Fletcher Allen, December 2, 2010, https://www.youtube.com/watch?v=yHYejTZh_0I.

7. Melinda Estes, MD, *Healthy Food in Health Care,* YouTube video, 5:30-5:55, posted by Fletcher Allen, December 2, 2010, https://www.youtube.com/watch?v=yHYejTZh_0I.

8. Melinda Estes, MD, *Healthy Food in Health Care,* YouTube video, 6:19-6:50, posted by Fletcher Allen, December 2, 2010, https://www.youtube.com/watch?v=yHYejTZh_0I.

Part 3 Introduction

1. Emma Thomas, "'Exhausted' Merrill Lynch Intern Died from Epileptic Fit in Shower after He 'Pulled Three All-Nighters at Bank Where Employees Compete to Work the Longest Hours,'" *Mail Online,* November 22, 2013, http://www.dailymail.co.uk/news/article 2511911/Moritz-Erhardt-exhausted-Merrill-Lynch-intern-died-epileptic-fit.html.

2. Suza Scalora, "An Interview with Arianna Huffington," *Eckhart Teachings,* May 2014, http://communicate.eckharttolle.com/news/2014/05/09/an-interview-with-arianna-huffington-by-suza-scalora/.

Chapter 7

1. Author interview with a public safety professional, October 2, 2014.

2. Edgar Schein, interview by author, audio recording, August 15, 2014.

3. "Barry-Wehmiller—Our History," Barry-Wehmiller Companies, August 20, 2014, http://www.barrywehmiller.com/our-business/our-history.

4. Aviv Shahar, interview by author, audio recording, September 18, 2014.

5. Martyn Drake, interview by author, e-mail correspondence, October 13, 2014.

6. Martyn Drake, interview by author, e-mail correspondence, October 13, 2014.

7. *The Growing Impact of Wage-and-Hour Regulations,* Express Employment Professionals, http://www.expresssrg.com/employers/resources/white%20paper/SRG12VU_WHITEPAPER_5USprint.pdf 3.

8. *The Growing Impact of Wage-and-Hour Regulations,* Express Employment Professionals, http://www.expresssrg.com/employers/resources/white%20paper/SRG12VU_WHITEPAPER_5USprint.pdf 3. 6.

9. *The Profit,* CNBC, http://www.cnbcprime.com/the-profit/. The Profit Amazing Grapes Wine Store, Season 2, Episode 207, Aired April 8, 2014.

10. Bruce Lipton, *The Biology of Belief: Unleashing the Power of Consciousness, Matter, & Miracles* (Carlsbad, CA: Hay House, 2007).

11. Bruce Lipton, *The Biology of Belief: Unleashing the Power of Consciousness, Matter, & Miracles* (Carlsbad, CA: Hay House, 2007), 16.

12. Bruce Lipton, *The Biology of Belief: Unleashing the Power of Consciousness, Matter, & Miracles* (Carlsbad, CA: Hay House, 2007), 16.

13. Bruce Lipton, *The Biology of Belief: Unleashing the Power of Consciousness, Matter, & Miracles* (Carlsbad, CA: Hay House, 2007), 17.

14. Stacey Peterson and Joe Chinn, interview by author, audio recording, August 13, 2014.

15. Stacey Peterson, interview by author, audio recording, August 13, 2014.

16. Nikki Sells, interview by author, audio recording, August 5, 2014.

17. *Guiding Principles of Leadership,* Barry-Wehmiller Companies, September 1, 2014, http://www1.barry-wehmiller.com/docs/shareddocuments/gpl_document.pdf.

18. Bob Chapman, "Walk Your Talk," *Bob Chapman's Truly Human Leadership Blog,* December 5, 2012, http://www.trulyhumanleadership.com/?p=356.

Chapter 8

1. Denise Bredfeldt, interview by author, audio recording, September 18, 2014.

2. Lauren Dixon, interview by author, audio recording, July 22, 2014.

3. Daniel Pink, *A Whole New Mind: Why Right-Brainers Will Rule the Future* (New York: Riverhead Trade, 2006).

4. Daniel Pink, *Drive: The Surprising Truth About What Motivates Us,* (New York: Riverhead Trade, 2011).

5. Daniel Pink, "The Puzzle of Motivation," TEDGlobal 2009, July 2009, 9:15, http://www.ted.com/talks/dan_pink_on_motivation#t-548054.

6. Edgar Schein, interview by author, audio recording, August 15, 2014.

7. Denise Bredfeldt, interview by author, audio recording, September 18, 2014.

8. Denise Bredfeldt, interview by author, audio recording, September 18, 2014.

9. Lauren Dixon, interview by author, audio recording, July 22, 2014.

Chapter 9

1. Bob Chapman, "Defining Moments," Barry-Wehmiller, YouTube, March 12, 2012, 12:40-14:10, https://www.youtube.com/watch?v=k3w ZpeVkxZo.

2. Bob Chapman, "Defining Moments," Barry-Wehmiller, YouTube, March 12, 2012, 18:06, https://www.youtube.com/watch?v=k3wZpeVkxZo.

3. Paul Green, interview by author, audio recording, August 12, 2014.

4. Stacey Peterson, interview by author, audio recording, August 13, 2014.

5. Joe Chinn, interview by author, audio recording, August 13, 2014.

6. Rich Armstrong, interview by author, audio recording, September 23, 2014.

7. Peter Drucker, *Concept of the Corporation* (New Jersey: Transaction Publishers, 1993), 168.

8. Rich Armstrong, interview by author, audio recording, September 23, 2014.

9. Rich Armstrong, interview by author, audio recording, September 23, 2014.

10. "Ritz-Carlton Gold Standards," Ritz-Carlton Hotel Company, September 11, 2014, http://www.ritzcarlton.com/en/Corporate/Gold Standards/Default.htm.

11. Christine Daues and Joe Daues, interview by author, audio recording, August 15, 2014.

12. Christine Daues and Joe Daues, interview by author, audio recording, August 15, 2014.

13. Christine Daues and Joe Daues, interview by author, audio recording, August 15, 2014.

REFERENCES

Barry-Wehmiller Companies. "Barry-Wehmiller—Our History." http:// www.barrywehmiller.com/our-business/our-history. Accessed September 21, 2014.

Barry-Wehmiller Companies. *Guiding Principles of Leadership.* http:// www1.barry-wehmiller.com/docs/shareddocuments/gpl_document.pdf. Accessed September 21, 2014.

CBSnews.com. "Colo. Principal Says She Was Fired Over 'Disrespectful' Policy Towards Poor Children." CBSnews.com, January 8, 2014. http://www.cbsnews.com/news/former-colo-principal-claims-fired-for -fighting-student-humiliation/.

Chapman, Bob. "Defining Moments." Barry-Wehmiller Companies. YouTube, March 12, 2012. https://www.youtube.com/watch?v=k3wZpeVkxZo.

Chapman, Bob. "Walk Your Talk." *Bob Chapman's Truly Human Leadership Blog,* December 5, 2012. http://www.trulyhumanleadership.com/?p=356.

Chism, Marlene. *Stop Workplace Drama: Train Your Team to Have No Complaints, No Excuses, and No Regrets.* New York: John Wiley and Sons, 2011.

Covey, Stephen. *The One Thing That Changes Everything.* New York: Free Press, 2008.

Deloitte Consulting LLP and Bersin by Deloitte. *Human Capital Trends Report for 2014.* http://www.deloitte.com/assets/Dcom-Namibia/Global HumanCapitalTrends2014_030714.pdf.

Drucker, Peter. *Concept of the Corporation.* New Jersey: Transaction Pub- lishers, 1993.

Drucker, Peter F. "Managing Knowledge Means Managing Oneself." *Leader to Leader* 16 (Spring 2000). http://rlacxp.com/studio/biz/conceptual _resources/authors/peter_drucker/mkmmo_org.pdf.

Estes, Melinda, MD. *Healthy Food in Health Care.* YouTube video, posted December 2, 2010. https://www.youtube.com/watch?v=yHYejTZh_0I.

References

Express Employment Professionals. *Top Five Threats Facing Business Today.* Accessed link from ExpressPros.com on September 8, 2014.

Express Employment Professionals. *The Growing Impact of Wage-and-Hour Regulations.* Accessed link from ExpressPros.com on September 8, 2014.

Fritz, Robert. *Path of Least Resistance: Learning to Become the Creative Force in Your Own Life,* revised and expanded edition. New York: Ballantine Books, 1989.

Griffo, Megan. "Doctor Walks 6 Miles Through Snow Storm to Perform Emergency Brain Surgery." *The Huffington Post,* January 31, 2014. http://www.huffingtonpost.com/2014/01/30/dr-zenko-hrynkiw-6-miles -brain-surgery_n_4697195.html.

Goldsmith, Marshall. "Try Feedforward Instead of Feedback." Adapted from *Leader to Leader,* Summer 2002. http://www.marshallgold smithlibrary.com/cim/articles_display.php?aid=110.

Goleman, Daniel. *Focus: The Hidden Driver of Excellence.* New York: Harper, 2013.

Haanel, Charles. *The Master Key System*, Manor Thrift Edition. Originally published 1912, reissued in this edition 2008.

Hill, Kashmir. "OfficeMax Blames Data Broker for 'Daughter Killed in Car Crash' Letter." Forbes.com, January 22, 2014. http://www.forbes .com/sites/kashmirhill/2014/01/22/officemax-blames-data-broker- for-daughter-killed-in-car-crash-letter/.

Kissel, Adam. "East Stroudsburg University Suspends Innocent Professor for Weeks over Facebook Comments." Foundation for Individual Rights in Education (FIRE), April 5, 2010. http://www.thefire.org/east-stroudsburg -university-suspends-innocent-professor-for-weeks-over-facebook -comments/.

Lipton, Bruce. *The Biology of Belief: Unleashing the Power of Consciousness, Matter, & Miracles*, revised edition. Carlsbad, California: Hay House, 2007.

Netscape editors. "No. 1 Reason People Quit Their Jobs." Accessed 2014. http://webcenters.netscape.compuserve.com/whatsnew/package.jsp? name=fte/quitjobs/quitjobs. Accessed September 7, 2014.

Nubile, Roberta. "Fletcher Allen's CEO Melinda Estes: No Soloist." *Vermont Woman,* April 2009. http://www.vermontwoman.com/articles/ 2009/0409/estes.html.

Pink, Daniel H. *A Whole New Mind: Why Right-Brainers Will Rule the Future.* New York: Riverhead Books, 2006.

References

Pink, Daniel H. *Drive: The Surprising Truth About What Motivates Us.* New York: Riverhead Books, 2011.

Pink, Daniel H. "The Puzzle of Motivation." TEDGlobal 2009, July 2009. http://www.ted.com/talks/dan_pink_on_motivation#t-548054.

Press Association. "Sir Bradley Wiggins Says Children Were Bullied Over Armstrong Drug Scandal." *Guardian* (U.K.), February 5, 2014. http://www.theguardian.com/sport/2014/feb/05/bradley-wiggings-lance-armstrong-children.

Ritz-Carlton Hotel Company. "Ritz-Carlton Gold Standards." http://www.ritzcarlton.com/en/Corporate/GoldStandards/Default.htm. Accessed August 24, 2014.

Rock, David. *Your Brain at Work: Strategies for Overcoming Distraction, Regaining Focus, and Working Smarter All Day Long.* New York: Harper Business, 2009.

Rozman, Deborah. "Heart Mastery." http://heartmastery.com/files/Deborah%20Rozman%20Bio.pdf. Accessed August 25, 2014.

Scalora, Suza. "An Interview with Arianna Huffington." *Eckhart Teachings,* May 2014. http://communicate.eckharttolle.com/news/2014/05/09/an-interview-with-arianna-huffington-by-suza-scalora/.

Schrotenboer, Brent. "Richie Incognito's Bully Reputation Goes Back to 2002." *USA Today,* November 5, 2013. http://www.usatoday.com/story/sports/nfl/2013/11/05/incognito-bully-accusations-nebraska-reshman/3439819/.

Senge, Peter. *The Fifth Discipline: The Art and Practice of the Learning Organization.* New York: Crown Publishing Group, 2006.

Smith, Emily Esfahani. "Social Connection Makes a Better Brain." *The Atlantic,* online edition, October 29, 2013. http://www.theatlantic.com/health/archive/2013/10/social-connection-makes-a-better-brain/280934/.

Sinek, Simon. "Why Leaders Eat Last." YouTube video, posted December 4, 2013, https://www.youtube.com/watch?v=ReRcHdeUG9Y.

Thomas, Emma. " 'Exhausted' Merrill Lynch Intern Died from Epileptic Fit in Shower after He 'Pulled Three All-Nighters at Bank Where Employees Compete to Work the Longest Hours.' " *Mail Online* (U.K.), November 22, 2013. http://www.dailymail.co.uk/news/article-2511911/Moritz-Erhardt-exhausted-Merrill-Lynch-intern-died-epileptic-fit.html.

Tolle, Eckhart. *The New Earth and Practicing the Power of Now: A Guide to Spiritual Enlightenment.* Novato, CA: New World Library, 2004.

USA Today. "Domestic Violence in Detail," *USA Today,* October 2, 2014.

References

Vaughan, Christopher. "Interview with Jack Stack." The Center for Ethics and Entrepreneurship, April 11, 2011. http://www.ethicsandentrepreneurship .org/20110411/interview-with-jack-stack/.

Yang, Jia Lynn, and Amrita Jayakumar. "Target Says Up to 70 Million More Customers Were Hit by December Data Breach." *Washington Post,* January 10, 2014. http://www.washingtonpost.com/ business/economy/target-says-70-million-customers-were-hit-by-dec-data-breach-more-than-first-reported/2014/01/10/0ada1026-79fe-11e3-8963-b4b654bcc9b2_story.html.

Zicconi, John. "Fletcher Allen's Ex-CEO Admits to Fraud." *Barre Montpelier Times Argus,* January 19, 2005. http://timesargus.com/apps/pbcs .dll/article?AID=/20050119/NEWS/501190337/1002.

ACKNOWLEDGMENTS

Authoring this book was an honor and a dream come true—a dream that could have never materialized without the support and encouragement of many people. No matter how much success a person has, you can go backwards and see the ripple effect of hundreds of people that had an influence on your success. For this book, I want to mention a few of the ripples.

I'm thankful that my parents brought me up to know God. This foundation created a platform for me to explore my relationship with the Divine, and to grow in spiritual understanding, which is a lifelong journey. It does not escape me how this blessing has provided the courage to introduce the concept of spiritual-awareness in a business book. Risky business, for sure, but one that I'm willing to take.

I'm thankful to my lifelong friends who have watched me transform from a blue collar factory worker to building the career of my dreams. The gap between where I started and where I am now was dark, wide, and full of doubts. Had it not been for those closest to me holding the light for me, encouraging me to take the next right step, and seeing more in me than I saw in myself, I might still be stacking a skid, packing cheese, and yelling "rotate!"

To Gerald, my husband of almost twenty-five years: You have seen most of my drama, and you're still here. It's not easy to marry a blue-collar factory girl who then decides to quit a job of twenty-one years to become an international professional speaker, author, and consultant. The career I've built is not necessarily one of convenience for you. From physically picking me up at inconvenient hours at the airport, to picking me up emotionally when I am anything but enlightened, I am grateful.

To the people at Sound View for your sound advice. While producing a video in your studio one of you asked me about my next book, which was just an idea. I said that my dream would be to work with a publisher that was out of the box—forward thinking, and would be a partner to me. You introduced me to Bibliomotion.

To Erika and Jill at Bibliomotion—Wow! You move fast! The two of you are the best No-Drama Leaders I have worked with. I'm grateful for your leadership, your mentoring, and your support. I'm grateful to the entire Bibliomotion team from cover design, to public relations, to editing. Thank you!

To the leaders who agreed to be interviewed for the book, I am most grateful to have met you and to have learned from your wisdom. You inspire me to see more and to be more.

To Heather Joyner, who started out as a client, became my first certified trainer, to becoming my executive assistant: Your dedication and tireless commitment to my work is a treasured gift. From making sure I didn't drop any balls, to listening to my ideas, to playing devil's advocate, to being my biggest cheerleader, I am truly grateful.

To you who reads this book, I'm thankful that our paths have crossed. I look forward to meeting you on a forum, a blog, webinar, a conference, or perhaps in your workplace.

INDEX

Index

Index

Index

Index

Index

Shahar, Aviv (world leader in strategic innovation), 121–122

shortening the gap concept, 89–90

silent treatment, 74

Simon, David (neurosurgeon), 30

social media, 65–66

Speed of Trust, The (Covey), 61

spiritual alignment, 13

spiritual awareness, 25–29

spiritual discomfort, 15

Stack, Jack (plant manager of International Harvester Renew Center), 79–81, 166

Stop Workplace Drama, 89

strategic communication, 66–72

Strategic Communication Model, 70–72

Super Vision, 62

T

Target, 101–102

teamwork, as sign of empowerment, 171

telling *versus* asking, 96–97

Thomas, Bryan, 7

Tolle, Eckhart
The New Earth and The Power of Now, 16

tools, as core element of accountability, 53–54

training opportunities, 50–51

transparency culture and, 11

trying on your values concept, 27–28

Turner, Jim, 10

turning a blind eye, 10–11

U

uncertainty, 87–88

unexpected and unwanted change, 86–87

unexpected but wanted change, 84–85

unwanted advice, 95–96

unwanted change and resistance, 90–94

V

values
aligning decisions with, 13–14
changing behavior to match, 28
competing, 16–17
declaring your, 14–16
that clash, 17–19
trying on your values concept, 27–28

values issues, 7–8

vision, as core element of accountability, 53

W

walking the talk, 6–7

well-being, signs of misalignment, 12–13

Whole New World, A (Pink), 141

Wiggins, Bradley, 17

willingness, 1–2

witness, as core element of accountability, 53–54

workplace relationships and communication, 60–61

Y

Your Brain at Work (Rock), 95

ABOUT THE AUTHOR

Marlene Chism is a consultant, international speaker, and the author of *Stop Workplace Drama: Train Your Team to Have No Complaints, No Excuses, and No Regrets.* Marlene's passion is developing wise leaders and helping people to discover, develop, and deliver their gifts to the world. Clients who work with Marlene report the following results: increased profitability through clarity and alignment, higher employee engagement, and dramatically improved workplace culture.

As an accomplished professional speaker with an international audience, Marlene is a dynamic storyteller with the ability to make the complex simple, engaging diverse audiences from corporate executives to entrepreneurs to frontline employees. She delivers her message on stopping drama and creating enlightened leaders through corporate retreats and client work, as well as at association meetings and other engagements.

Marlene has a communications degree from Drury University, and a master's degree from Webster University.

Web Resources
www.stopworkplacedrama.com
www.marlenechism.com

Contact Information:
1.888.434.9085
marlene@marlenechism.com